WOODY GUTHRIE

Unsung Americans

Woody Guthrie

A M E R I C A N   B A L L A D E E R

Janelle Yates

Ward Hill Press

U NSUNG A MERICANS

Other books in this series include:

Chief Joseph
Thunder Rolling Down From The Mountains

Dorothy Day
With Love for the Poor

Zora Neale Hurston
A Storyteller's Life

Table of Contents

Acknowledgments   7

1   "Crying Don't Help"   9

2   Town on a Hill   12

3   Railroad Blues   19

4   Ghost Town   23

5   Boom Town   27

6   Old-Fashioned Boy   31

7   Buried Treasure   34

8   I'm Going Where There's No Depression   37

9   Dust Pneumonia   41

10   Highway 66   44

11   Little Red Songbook   48

12   Lefty Lou   53

13   A New Deal   60

14   Woody Sez   66

15   The Big Time   72

16   Along the Green Valley   79

17   Railroad Pete   86

18   A Nautical Life   92

19   Boot Camp   97

20   Songs to Grow On   100

21   Walking the Lonesome Valley   106

22   "Go Back to Russia!"   108

23   Hard, Ain't It Hard   114

24   Green Pastures   118

Epilogue   124

Notes   127

Bibliography   132

Chronology   134

Publication Credits   138

Index   140

Acknowledgments

Thanks to Mark Maniak for all the books, recordings, articles and gently imparted knowledge. Thanks also to George Book, Lisa and Steve Carlson, Joe Doyle, Wilton Duckworth and Jim O'Grady.

Dr. Guy Logsdon of Tulsa, Oklahoma, was the source of several captivating telephone discussions and engrossing written materials. Pete Seeger was gracious enough to share some of his memories with me. And Harold Leventhal made time to discuss this project, answer questions and share his recollections of Woody Guthrie's last years. He also connected me to several important sources and made available most of the photos and all of the drawings in this book.

Bill Ochs served as a sounding board throughout this project. And his love and support made the writing easier.

"Crying Don't Help"

Woody Guthrie was playing in the tall grass outside his grandmother's farmhouse when the fire whistle began to blow one spring afternoon in 1919. As it wailed over the little town of Okemah, Oklahoma, Woody stood in the grass and listened. The whistle screamed high and low, high then low, repeating itself. Woody tried to count the number of times it wailed, to decipher its secret code, but after a few minutes the blasts trailed off and the afternoon grew quiet again. Yet Woody felt uneasy. He kept wondering where fire had hit. He just couldn't shake the sense of dread the siren had awakened in him.

A little while later, his older brother Roy showed up at the farm. He told Woody it was time to go, and he mentioned an accident. He said their sister Clara had been burned pretty badly and might not survive her injuries. Then he and another man drove Woody back to Okemah.

When they reached the Guthrie home, Woody found his parents weeping in the front rooms, while a throng of neighbors, relatives and townsfolk moved gently through the house. The air smelled faintly of smoke, and there were wet places on the floor. For a few long moments, Woody felt as though he had entered someone else's house. Everything looked so alien that he didn't know what to make of it. Then he began to listen to what the people were saying.

They were talking about Clara. Her dress had burst into flames that afternoon as she stood at the ironing board, and she had raced out the door and around the yard, screaming and burning, until a neighbor managed to smother the fire with a blanket. Most of the skin on her body had burned away. Now her temperature was dropping slowly, lower and lower, to dangerous levels. The doctor had already come and gone, offering little hope for her survival.

This sudden tragedy was almost more than six-year-old Woody could comprehend. For as long as he could remember he had loved and admired his older sister—a beautiful, spirited girl with gentle brown curls and vibrant eyes. When Clara sang along to her father's cowboy songs, Woody listened eagerly. And when she danced through the yard, her hair bouncing across her shoulders, Woody mimicked her movements. Their father, Charley Guthrie, spoiled Clara, buying her pretty trinkets and hauling her piggyback around the house. And though it wasn't always easy to get along with a fourteen-year-old, particularly one as headstrong as Clara, Nora Guthrie loved her daughter deeply.

Now the grief-stricken faces frightened Woody, and he fought the urge to run away and hide. Mustering his courage, he walked into Clara's room. His sister sat propped up in bed, her body wrapped in bandages. When she heard her brother enter, Clara turned and smiled brightly at him. "Hello there, old Mister Woodly," she called, using a pet name she had given him. Despite her condition, she seemed in good spirits, even strangely talkative. Woody didn't know what to say. This disaster had happened so fast—the fire whistle, Roy's jarring news and now Clara's cheerful bravery—that he could hardly speak for his fear and confusion. But Clara made him promise not to cry.

"It don't help...just makes everybody feel bad," she explained as Woody stood beside her bed, clamping down on the grief rising in the back of his throat. When she paused he nodded his head in agreement. He promised. Then Clara changed the subject and chatted warmly with the others. As the hours passed, she grew quieter and quieter, calmer and sleepier. Late in the evening she died peacefully, with seemingly little pain.

Nobody took it harder than Nora Guthrie, who blamed herself for her daughter's death. The two had quarreled, and she had kept Clara home from school that day, assigning her a list of chores, including the ironing. Now nothing and nobody could soothe Nora—not even for a moment. She talked about Clara constantly, pacing the house or wandering in a daze around Okemah. She neglected her other children, including little George, Woody's younger brother, and abandoned most of her housework. If only she had been more understanding with Clara! If only they hadn't quarreled! It was as though the flames still jumped and crackled in her mind, and she just couldn't put them out.

Woody was frightened by this turn of events. Although his mother had been acting strangely for some time now, she had always managed to take care of them, and her tenderness toward her family had never wavered. But now she seemed out of control, completely overcome with grief and guilt. To make matters worse, most of the townsfolk held her responsible for the accident. They had observed her erratic behavior and, for the most part, held their tongues, but now rumors about Nora sprouted like weeds. They said she had poured coal oil on Clara, that she had burned her new house down ten years earlier, before Woody was even born. And when she walked through the town, the stares and the gossip followed her every step.

Woody felt overwhelmed. There was a hole in the family where Clara had been, and now his mother seemed to be leaving too — in mind and spirit if not flesh. "For a while it looked like trouble had made us closer," he recalled. "But before long it was plainer than ever that it had been the breaking point for my mother." She seemed to have difficulty telling objects from people, in determining exactly who was present in the room with her. Sometimes her muscles would convulse, or she would begin to yell at the furniture or walls — or nothing in particular — her voice loud enough to carry several houses away. And Woody's father was broken-hearted, crying frequently about Clara and worrying over his wife. Finally he decided to move the family away from daily reminders of the accident, hoping a new home would restore Nora's fragile mental health.

Woody helped prepare for the move as best he could, but it didn't make much sense to him. He hardly recognized his family lately, and now they were leaving the home they had all shared. What would happen to them? Would his mother get better? And why did Clara have to die? But he pondered these questions silently. His father never talked about their troubles, and Woody had promised Clara he'd be brave.

CHAPTER 2

Town on a Hill

few weeks later the Guthries moved to a small farm several miles from Okemah. It was calmer there, away from the watchful eyes of the townsfolk, but Nora's condition grew steadily worse. She was agitated and scattered most of the time, prone to fits of crying or yelling. Woody felt lonely for Clara. And he missed the old house with its second-floor veranda, where he had looked out over a wide expanse of Okemah, past the street at the bottom of the hill all the way to the rail yards, where engineers hitched and unhitched their cargo, giving short shrill blasts on the whistle. Sometimes he could even see the farmers heading to town, their wagons loaded with cotton for the mill. Now he lived away from town and he missed it, though not nearly as much as he missed his sister.

The town of Okemah was young then. The Fort Smith and Western railroad ran through it, and the Canadian River threaded past only a few miles to the south. Okemah hoped to attract another railroad to its hilltop in the eastern half of the state, and with it a lot more inhabitants than the fifteen hundred or so who lived there when Woody was growing up. The streets were wide and unpaved, and the horses, mule-drawn wagons, and automobiles that pounded through them each day kicked up a haze of dust. A sudden downpour transformed the roads into gooey muck. And on Saturdays, when the farmers came into town to trade, the streets grew boisterous — and even dustier.

But long before the farmers and the townsfolk had arrived, and centuries before Oklahoma won statehood, Native Americans roamed across these plains, following the buffalo that sustained

The Okemah house in which Woody grew up.

them. The Arapaho, Caddo, Cheyenne and other tribes traveled through the territory when the hunt required it, though most of these Indians came from other regions of the west, and Oklahoma remained largely uninhabited. In the 1820s, the U.S. government forced five Southeastern tribes to move from their homelands around Florida to the eastern half of the state—a mix of flat grasslands, gentle hills and sandstone ridges that had been designated as "Indian Territory." The Choctaws, Cherokees, Chickasaws, Creeks and Seminoles were often called the Five *Civilized* Tribes because they had long associated with whites and borrowed many of their customs.

Although the U.S. government gave the five tribes a treaty and promised that the Oklahoma territory would belong to them "as long as grass shall grow and rivers run," it seized a large section of their lands after the Civil War and opened them to the white homesteaders creeping westward across America. Before long there were more whites than Indians. Farms and small towns sprang up across the territory, most of them owned and governed by whites. The Indians still held property in the region, and many had been slave holders before the Civil War, but most were exploited by the whites with whom they traded. And the African Americans of the area still lived in extreme poverty, barred from voting by a literacy requirement few could meet, and were limited to work in fields and kitchens or at other low-paying, dead-end jobs.

It was 1907 when Charley Guthrie first arrived in Okemah, having just been elected District Clerk. A handsome, intelligent man brimming with energy and ambition (he read law books in his spare time), he hoped for a long and distinguished career in politics. He loved to box and tell wild stories from his cowboy days in Texas. The men in town were drawn by his raucous charm and entertaining ways, but their wives remained a little wary. And long before Clara's death they had raised their eyebrows over Nora, too, finding her behavior a little mannish for their tastes — like when she went galloping across the countryside on horseback, singing as she flew along.

When Woody was born on July 14, 1912, his politically minded father named him Woodrow Wilson Guthrie — after the man recently nominated for president of the United States. But from the start, everyone just called him Woody. He felt secure in Okemah, where all the townsfolk were well-acquainted (and knew everyone's business, both public and private) and where talking seemed to be the primary pastime. The women bragged about their children, compared recipes and discussed the progress of cotton and other crops. The men talked farming and weather and politics every morning at the local drugstore, where Charley was popular. When Clara was alive, the Guthrie house was usually full of singing, though Nora preferred the Irish and English ballads she'd learned from her mother to the rowdy songs her husband liked to sing. She smiled at the little rhymes Woody invented and listened intently to the stories he concocted, her dark eyes lit with interest and

Charley and Nora Guthrie, c. 1917 (Courtesy Mary Jo Guthrie Edgmon).

amusement. There were enough kids Woody's age to keep him busy playing war or sneaking into storm cellars to sample the pickles and peaches and knobby cucumbers from cool glass jars that sweated in stony darkness. They'd chase each other through barns and backyards and climb tall, leafy trees. And they'd watch the townsfolk ready themselves for the Saturday night dances — the women donning clean dresses and ribbons, the men with freshly shined slick-soled shoes, the teenagers eyeing one another nervously. There was usually a fiddler providing the music, often a guitar player or two.

Charley on horseback, Okemah
(Courtesy Mary Jo Guthrie Edgmon).

Woody was too young for the dancing, but he loved music all the same. And though he grew up in the years before radio and television — even before many folks had records or phonographs — his childhood was steeped in music: his mother's mournful ballads, sung in her twangy, high-pitched voice, and Charley's cowboy songs, which made Woody's ears "stand away out and wiggle for more." The whine of the trains passing through town made music, too, punctuated with thick spirals of smoke. On quiet afternoons, the wind played soft notes in the leaves of the trees while the insects sawed along behind it. And sometimes a dog would howl in the distance, like a far-off violin. In the evenings, when Charley called to the horses as he headed down the clay road toward home, "it sounded like a song" to Woody. And "when he would call the purebred pigs, sows, shoats and boars, his voice was as much of a song in the air as [there] ever was. And when the mare was led into the lot gate, the neigh and nicker of the stud was a song as soft as a mating pigeon."

Over time, Woody adjusted to life on the farm. It had its good side. He liked being around the animals his father bred, the hogs and

Woody with his parents and younger brother George, early 1920s.

the horses and the bitter smells of the pens where they stayed. In the fall and winter there was wood smoke in the air. And in the spring, after a good rain, the scent of damp earth filled his nostrils. He rode into town with his father as often as he could. And sometimes his grandmother, Mary Tanner, stopped by to visit and held him in her sturdy arms. He liked spending time at her farmhouse, too, where "everything was nice, new and pretty," he remembered, including the piano in the front room where his mother would sometimes sit and play. For years the Tanner farm had been one of Nora Guthrie's favorite places. But now she seemed only half-conscious of it, and her behavior became so unpredictable that Lee Tanner, her stepfather, began discouraging her visits.

Meanwhile, Okemah was booming. Oil was discovered nine miles east of town, then to the south and west. In fact, "there was a whole big ocean of oil laying under" the state, Woody wrote. Since a railroad ran through Okemah, the town became a hub of activity. In a matter of weeks its population exploded to ten thousand people as oil field workers, land speculators and assorted hangers-on mobbed the town. "Pretty soon the creeks around Okemah was filled with black scum," he recalled, "and the rivers flowed with it, so that it looked like a stream of rainbow-colored gold drifting hot along the waters." During the blistering days of summer, the oil added a new smell to the landscape — petroleum fumes — discernible "for miles and miles in every direction."

Land was selling like crazy now, all around Okemah. A fortune could be made overnight if a person knew how to handle the big deals. For years Charley had made a good living in the real estate business, but now he began to lose money. And no matter what he did, he couldn't seem to regain his touch. He was tired and slow-moving, with a sadness in his eyes that was painful to behold. While everyone around him was enjoying new prosperity, Charley was slowly going broke.

On top of that, his hands began to bother him. They grew stiff and sore with arthritis, from all his brawls and boxing matches, he guessed. By the end of the day, his fingers would coil into tight, painful fists. Woody and his older brother Roy took turns massaging them when they could, but it didn't help much. "He had to go to a doctor and have the little finger on his left hand cut off," Woody remembered, "because the muscles drawed it down so hard against the palm of his hand that the fingernail cut a big hole into his flesh."

In early 1922, Nora gave birth to a daughter, named Mary Josephine. Charley had hoped another child might soothe his wife and help ease the pangs of Clara's death, but the baby seemed to have little effect. Later that year, Charley decided to run for political office again, thinking a win would jump-start his faltering career, but he lost by a huge margin. Desperate for money, he tried selling fire extinguishers, but nobody was buying. Finally he moved his family away from Okemah altogether, to a small house in Oklahoma City.

And then it began to appear as though Nora might recover. Her mind seemed to focus again. She planted a small garden and resumed her cooking and cleaning, and carried on conversations in a normal tone of voice. Roy got a job pumping gas, and Woody and Charley delivered milk and groceries, but even with three people working the family barely scraped by. At night Charley's hands ached more than ever, sometimes so badly he couldn't get to sleep unless one of the boys massaged his fingers.

"I'd hold both of his hands under the covers and rub them," Woody remembered, "and feel the gristle on his knuckles, swelled up four times natural size, and the cemented muscles under each finger." Life had gotten hard for them all, so hard Woody often felt like weeping, but he didn't. He remembered his promise to Clara and, choking back his sadness, did his best to help his family.

A few months after the move to Oklahoma City, Nora's stepbrother, Leonard Tanner, showed up in town. He'd been offered a chance to run a big motorcycle dealership, and he wanted Charley to handle the bookkeeping end of the business. Charley was elated. Life had been pretty bleak, and this new job might finally turn things around. But before they could work out all the details, Leonard was killed in a motorcycle accident, and the dealership went to somebody else.

CHAPTER 3

Railroad Blues

kemah's boom ended. The oil field workers and the opportunists moved on to other communities, and the streets regained their small-town quiet. When Charley and his family returned from Oklahoma City in the summer of 1924, many Okcmah residents who had profited from the boom were careful to steer clear of him, lest his failures be contagious. He moved his family into an abandoned boomer shack on the town's east side—the poor side—squeezing their belongings into two rickety rooms with a tiny kitchen added on one end of the structure. It was like no place Woody had ever lived before, and it fascinated and saddened him at the same time. "Maybe it had housed somebody, lots of people, before we come," he wrote, "but it never had got a coat of paint. The rain rotted the shingles and the ground rotted the bottom boards, and the middle had just warped and twisted itself into fits trying to hold together....And the whole yard was running wild with weeds and wild flowers, brittle and sticky and covered with a fine sifting dust that lifted and fell from the highway."

Nora's mental state continued to fluctuate. For a while she would seem as normal as anybody else, scrubbing the filth out of the floorboards and walls, singing as she went along. But then a change would come over her. The light in her eyes would slowly go out, like a door swinging shut, and her breathing would accelerate. She seemed transported to another place and time, panic-stricken and lost. Woody and Roy tried their best to watch out for her, doing the cooking and cleaning and looking after the younger children, but most of the time it was more than they could handle.

When his mother was calm, Woody liked to wander the streets

of Okemah. Now that all the oil field folks were gone, it was smaller and tamer, and he missed the excitement. Sometimes the town seemed so quiet it had a ghost-like quality to it, although most of its original inhabitants remained. As he drifted through Okemah, Woody noticed weeds and grass poking through the sidewalks, scraps of garbage blowing down the quiet streets, and boarded-up store windows. One afternoon, as he was ambling past the barber shop, he heard a snatch of music and paused to look inside. A young black man, who earned his living shining shoes in the shop, was leaning back in a chair playing a harmonica. The music he was making was "the lonesomest piece of music" Woody had ever heard, and he stayed to listen. As soon as he got a chance, he asked the man where he had learned it.

The man called the tune the "Railroad Blues" and said he was imitating the whine of the trains that passed through Okemah. Woody went back to the shop many times after that, but the man "never did play the same piece no two days alike, and he called them all the 'Railroad Blues.'" Soon after, Woody got himself a harmonica and started tinkering with it. It helped take his mind off his troubles. Before long, he had figured out some simple tunes.

At home, Nora went in and out of her "spells," usually with little advance warning. Sometimes — but it was becoming increasingly rare — she seemed so calm and unafflicted that Woody had "a feeling in me that I had been hunting for the bigger part of my life. A wide-open feeling that she was just like any other boy's mama." He longed to capture that sensation, to fix it so that his family could finally get past the hard times and worries that had plagued them for so many years now. But Nora's mind would drift off again, and Woody and Roy would busy themselves trying to protect and distract her.

Eventually Charley found a job as a bookkeeper, then as a county employee distributing licenses, but his health was getting worse, too. He was in pain most of the time from the arthritis, and suffered frequent bouts of depression over his inability to provide for his family. Nora's behavior was also taking its toll. He missed her quiet alertness, her tenderness. Lately she was always angry or frightened about something, with physical lapses that scared the whole family. If it weren't for Roy and Woody looking after her, he didn't know what would happen to them all.

The local theater, where they ran the latest motion pictures, became an unexpected haven, and Nora and her sons started going regularly. In the darkened movie house, nobody stared at them the way they did in the streets and shops, and the stories enacted on the screen helped Nora forget her own sad life. She developed a special fondness for a slender, clown-like actor named Charlie Chaplin, who played a character called "the Tramp," a battered little man with a funny walk and baggy pants. He had an open, innocent face, loose strands of dark hair that drifted across his forehead, and an abbreviated moustache that made him look sweet instead of sinister. Although he was obviously very poor, he always wore gloves and a derby hat, and he carried a cane to show he had dignity. Woody loved him as much as his mother did, especially the easygoing way he faced each new challenge, and he felt a subtle sadness every time the screen faded to stillness at the end of a movie.

In 1926, things got so bad at home that Charley sent the two youngest children, George and Mary Jo, to live with his sister Maude in Texas. Nora was no longer capable of caring for them. She was always flustered and agitated and, when Charley was around the house, belligerent and accusing, too. People were beginning to suggest that Charley commit her to an asylum, but he balked at the idea. He "still believed that he could start out on a peanut hull and fight his way back into the ten-thousand-dollar oil deals, the farms, the ranchlands, the royalties, and the leases," Woody wrote. And with a little money, he'd be able to get Nora the care she needed. Even so, he avoided going home as much as possible and, as Nora grew more erratic, so did Woody and Roy.

Woody started hanging around with drifters on the edge of town — migrant workers, unemployed men and alcoholics, mostly. He'd listen to their stories and songs, help them scavenge for food and collect scraps of metal and other garbage to sell for spare change. He started playing hookey from school, too, which seemed dull compared to the rest of his life. The other kids made fun of him because he was small and because his hair was curly and — most stinging of all — because of his family troubles. When he did show up for classes, he spent most of his time writing stories and drawing stick-figure cartoons — two of his favorite pastimes. On Saturdays, when the farmers and the Indians came to town to trade, he sometimes played his harmonica and danced.

In the spring of 1927, just when it seemed as though things

couldn't get any worse, Charley lost his job. He was not yet fifty, but looked much older — with hunched shoulders, a shriveled face and swollen, twisted hands. And he felt the way he looked: worn-out and despondent. One afternoon, while he was napping, he suddenly caught fire and was badly burned from his neck to his waist. The local newspaper reported that he'd been doused with kerosene before the fire ignited. They didn't say it, but the most obvious assailant would have been Nora. But Charley refused to explain how he'd gotten burned. Hospitalized and unable to care for his family, he was forced to make a decision about his wife. He couldn't leave her on her own anymore, and Woody and Roy were too young to shoulder the burden without him. The next day he arranged her commitment to a mental hospital in Norman, Oklahoma, more than sixty miles away. But Woody was visiting the Tanner farm when they took his mother away, and wasn't home to say goodbye.

Ghost Town

hile Charley languished in the hospital, Woody and Roy fended for themselves in the little shack. The family's disintegration had been difficult for both sons to bear, but they reacted to it in different ways. During the day, Roy worked as a grocery clerk, while Woody roamed through the town. Roy worked hard and saved his money, spending it wisely on clean clothes and meals. Woody rarely bathed or combed his hair anymore, and his clothes were usually torn and smeared with dirt. And he didn't seem to care a whit about what the townspeople thought of him.

But the brothers had identical reactions to the shack: They hated it. Despite the repairs the family had made, the place continued to fall apart, and neither son had the energy to cook or clean. There were just too many bad memories hovering in those small rooms. "It seemed like everything in the world echoed in there," Woody later wrote. "I know how I felt about it, I only had one feeling toward it: I wanted to get the hell out of it."

When Charley was released from the hospital, still in such bad shape he was unable to care for himself, he decided to join his younger children in Texas. Woody and Roy accompanied him to the train station and watched as he was carried on board on a stretcher. They said their goodbyes to him as the train pulled out and listened as its whistle interrupted the quiet afternoon. Woody was barely fifteen.

He knew he couldn't expect Roy to look after him. At twenty-one, Roy was scarcely a man himself, so Woody wasn't too surprised when he moved into a rooming house shortly after Charley's departure. A few families offered to take in Woody, but he wasn't interested. Since the beginning of his mother's illness, he'd looked after himself more and more of the time. He'd learned to cherish his independence, and he disliked having to follow other people's rules. Besides, he knew where to get free bread (the local baker gave it to him) and the choicest scraps of food. And now, with his harmonica and his dancing, he was able to earn his own money, too. He simply picked a spot in town and started hopping about to his music. People would gather, smiles spreading across their faces, and toss their coins into his hat.

There was a tiny tin shack in Okemah that Woody and a few other boys had adopted as their "hideout." Soon after Charley's departure, Woody began sleeping there, too. It wasn't very comfortable. Now that it was summer, the weather was steamy hot. Even so, in many ways, Woody's life seemed calmer than it had in a while. He hadn't realized what a toll his mother's illness and his father's long decline had taken. But now that the daily struggles had ended, Woody felt more hopeful about the future, though he missed his mother terribly and still had awful nightmares sometimes.

During the day, Woody and the other members of his "gang"— about thirteen boys altogether—had plenty to keep them occupied. There was swimming in the Canadian River, as well as hiking and fishing and climbing trees. They would often invent some drama to act out. "We elected our own sheriff and deputy sheriff...and the rest of us, you know, we'd be the outlaws," Woody remembered. (The "sheriff had to have somebody to throw in jail," he explained.) "We had a nice little jail built out of a piano box" with bed slats nailed across it. Other times the boys aped their elders—concocting big pots of "moonshine" or bootleg whiskey—but the results were usually more nauseating than intoxicating.

Months passed, and the weather got cold. Woody began to suffer in the hideout, with only a worn-out blanket and his clothes to keep him warm. When it got too cold to sleep there, Casper Moore— one of his gang buddies—convinced Woody to move in with him. The Moores didn't have much money. They'd followed the oil boom to Okemah, and when it had gone, so had their prosperity. But they were friendly people who welcomed their new housemate without hesitation.

Casper's father, Tom, played the fiddle and soon found an eager musical partner in Woody, who could now twang a jaw harp and slap out rhythms on a pair of carved animal bones. Tom and Woody played and sang together most evenings during the winter of 1927-28, often with the family joining in. When they couldn't remember the verses to a song, Woody would make up a new set on the spur of the moment, with no need for pencil and paper. When he was feeling down or just wanted to talk, Nonie Moore, Casper's mother, proved to be a sympathetic listener. And though the house was crowded and money scarce, Woody felt glad to be there. The Moores treated him like a regular member of the family, and their acceptance eased the mistrust he often felt for other people.

But Casper's father grew restless. Okemah had ceased to thrive, and Tom Moore was hungry for new opportunities. He began to talk of other places, most of them far away, and soon decided to leave the state. He invited Woody to come along, but Woody wasn't interested. He felt uneasy about traveling too far from home. He did ask Tom to take him to the town of Norman before he left. For some time now, Woody had been eager to see his mother again. But when he arrived at the mental hospital and made his way to the dim, dismal room in which Nora waited, he almost regretted the trip. It took his mother forever to figure out who he was. Her physical symptoms were much worse, too, and the shock was almost more than Woody could bear. The doctors said something about a disease called Huntington's, but Woody didn't know what it was, and there was obviously no cure.

The Moores left Okemah a few weeks later, and Woody was on his own again. He quickly reverted to his old routines, but the town felt hollow, as though it had no heart anymore. As the summer of 1929 approached, and the weather grew increasingly reliable, Woody packed up his few belongings and headed south to Texas. He aimed to make it to the Gulf of Mexico, where some old friends now lived. He wasn't sure exactly how he would get there, but he wasn't too worried about it. He would soon be seventeen years old. He knew how to take care of himself.

Every day, Woody would stand out on the highway with his thumb in the air, hitching rides a little further south. And every night he'd stop in the nearest town and look for the railroad yard, where he knew he'd find a bunch of people camped—migrant workers, mostly, who had to travel to earn a living. They took jobs picking crops and moved across the country with the different harvests, from cotton in the central plains of Texas to the magnificent vistas of wheat lining the Great Plains all the way to Canada. In the camps Woody would find food and — more importantly — music and conversation. He would eat quickly and then sit back to listen, taking in the drawl of the voices and all the songs and stories they shared.

In a few days, Woody made it to Galveston, Texas, and looked out over the ocean for the first time in his life. He located his friends from Oklahoma, but lost his enthusiasm about visiting them when he discovered that they expected him to work. He wandered a while longer, then headed back home to Okemah. A letter from Charley awaited his return, beckoning Woody to Pampa, Texas, where Charley had recently taken a job. Woody set out at once, traveling due west to the northern plains of the Texas panhandle, where Pampa was situated on a high plateau.

CHAPTER 5

Boom Town

T he wind was always blowing in Pampa, or so it seemed to Woody. Sometimes its breezes caressed the town, like a whisper, and sometimes they raged with incredible force. The weather was still warm when he arrived, the ground lined with tawny grasses, the sky huge and blue and seemingly endless.

Pampa was in the throes of an oil boom even more ferocious than the one that had hit Okemah a few years earlier. Some of the world's richest stores of petroleum and natural gas had been discovered beneath the Texas panhandle — and Pampa, like other communities in the region, was reeling from the effects. The town was "wilder than a woodchuck," Woody recalled. Its population had skyrocketed, leaving the wealthier north side of town relatively unaffected but crowding the south side with row upon row of dilapidated shacks, where the oil field workers and other newcomers lived. The homes there weren't built to last very long, Woody explained, "because the big majority of the working folks will walk into town, work like a horse for a while, put the oil wells in...get the oil to flowing steady and easy into the rich people's tanks....and [then] move along down the road, as broke, as down and out, as tough, as hard hitting, as hard working, as the day they come to town."

The rooming house where Charley worked was a long, flimsy, two-story structure made out of tin. Charley had a small, modest bedroom to himself and an even sparser office. His job was to collect rent from the oil field workers who slept on the cots downstairs — and from the prostitutes who occupied the private cubicles upstairs. He seemed genuinely happy to see Woody again. It had been almost two years since they had parted, and he had worried often about his son. Charley's burns had healed well enough for him to move around and look after himself, but his overall health was still poor. He looked and acted much older than his fifty years, yet was still a great believer in a man's ability to improve himself regardless of the circumstances. He had high hopes for Woody.

Woody quickly made himself at home and got to know as many of the boarders as he could, though the cot-renters rarely stayed for more than eight or nine hours before heading back out to the oil fields. And he did visit the girls upstairs, who treated him more like a younger brother than a potential customer, although most of them were hardly older than he was. Soon Woody had lined the walls with cartoons and sketches, which eased the dreariness of the place, but only a little.

A seventeen-year-old needed money, just like anybody else, so Woody took a job across the street from the rooming house, behind the counter of Harris Drug. For three dollars a day he would sell root beer to any customers who came along, and he would supply bottles "of another description" to customers expressly requesting them. Since alcoholic beverages had been declared illegal in 1919 — when Prohibition was enacted — the demand for moonshine had skyrocketed, and Harris Drug did a whopping business at $1.50 a bottle, as Woody soon discovered. Whenever there was a lull in business, he drew cartoons or poked around the store. One day he found an old guitar and started fooling around with it. "I thought it sounded awful pretty," he recalled. After a while, he figured out a few simple chords and then "a few little old songs." He also started hanging around his Uncle Jeff Guthrie, Charley's younger half-brother and one of the best old-time fiddle players in the Texas panhandle. Jeff and his wife Allene, who played accordion, loved music better than anything and fancied having a show business career one day. They were more than happy to have Woody around as an excuse to perform, and soon he was spending all his spare time in their tiny apartment, learning chords and playing along as best he could on the old guitar.

But Charley worried about his son. All Woody seemed to care about was playing music or drawing silly cartoons. He didn't seem at all concerned about the future — about earning a living, that is. He certainly couldn't sell bootleg whiskey for the rest of his life! So Charley began pressuring Woody to go back to high school and earn a diploma, and finally Woody agreed to try.

From left: Matt Jennings, Woody, and an unidentified youth, Pampa, Texas, c. 1930.

But he detested school. Though he loved books and had always been curious about the world around him, he found his classes dull. Part of the problem was his independence. He was accustomed to going wherever he pleased and to feeding his whims, no matter how ridiculous they might seem to others. He'd rather pass the time in the local library reading books that actually interested him than have some teacher assign several boring chapters in a textbook. He also felt different from most of the other students — and the truth was, he was different, having faced a string of hardships at a young age. The football players made fun of his size, and many others considered him odd. He lasted a couple of semesters, then dropped out again — this time for good. But he did make one friend — a tall, redheaded loner like himself named Matt Jennings, who shared Woody's curiosity and love of music. Matt had recently bought an old fiddle and was trying to learn how to play it, so Woody hauled him over to Jeff and Allene's, where Matt became a regular, too.

Though they played different instruments, the boys were at the same level musically, struggling to learn the basic chords, technique and rhythms that would one day — they hoped — make them as good as Uncle Jeff. They started sneaking into old-time dances to listen to the string bands, which they preferred to the more popular — and more modern — dance orchestras. The modern groups played smooth, polished versions of waltzes and other fancy dances, but the string bands whooped it up with reels and other lively tunes, some with simple lyrics known to all the dancers. One of Woody's favorites was a tune called "Old Joe Clark" with a chorus especially suited to square dancing:

> *Round and round old Joe Clark*
> *Goodbye Betty Brown*
> *Round and round old Joe Clark*
> *I'm gonna leave this town*

After the Saturday night dances, Woody and Matt worked even harder at their instruments, often sitting for hours without talking, just playing along together on the tunes they were learning. But they entertained themselves in other ways, too — by swimming, shooting at cans and bottles, and drinking anything that might produce the wooziness of liquor. Matt's presence softened Woody. After a long drought, here was friendship again — possibly the first close friendship of his lifetime. The two spent long evenings and nights talking (Woody did most of the talking while Matt listened), playing music, and just hanging around. A degree of trust sprang up between them that Woody had never known before. Woody confided to Matt what he had never talked about before: his mother's illness and his sister's fire. And Woody turned to Matt when he got the news of his mother's death, in late 1929. Matt just listened quietly, as he always did — a trait Woody found soothing. But the truth was, Nora's death pained Woody more deeply than he could express to anyone for many years. "Somewhere on the outskirts of town, a high, whining fire whistle seemed to be blowing," he later wrote, recalling the day he heard of her passing.

CHAPTER 6

Old-Fashioned Boy

n late 1929, the stock market plummeted, and the country broke into a panic. As a new decade dawned, millions of workers lost their jobs, thousands of farmers abandoned or were evicted from their land, and businesses and banks closed their doors and ceased operations. Yet Woody continued as before, relatively unaffected. Since he had never been a regular member of the work force or had much money to spend, his life hardly changed at all — at first. He just kept focusing on his music, eventually forming a group called the Corncob Trio with Matt and a guitar player named Cluster Baker. The music they played was distinctly old-style: reels, barn dances, breakdowns and other square-dance tunes.

Many of the other young people in Pampa modeled themselves after their peers in the big cities and preferred the jazz and orchestra music that played there. They hoped to escape their rural roots, which seemed ordinary and not at all glamorous, especially when compared to the cosmopolitan lifestyles of places like New York and Chicago. But Woody and his friends loved the powerful whine of a fiddle as it sailed into an old tune like "Sourwood Mountain" with the guitar's steady strum behind it. And the airy staccato of the banjo was just about as satisfying. In this sense, they were more like their parents and grandparents, who had grown up in the years before radio.

Although phonographs had appeared on the scene in the late 1880s, only certain types of music ever made it onto records before 1920, and these were mostly pop and classical pieces. To hear old-time tunes, folks had to travel to dance halls and other places where live musicians gathered. But in the 1920s, with the advent of radio, that began to change. The new medium brought popular music to small towns and connected people across the country in ways that had seemed inconceivable a few short years before. Stations that reached rural areas or farming communities began making a special effort to provide their listeners with the "hillbilly" sound. Live musicians were hired to play over the air for an extended period of time. Some of these programs became so popular that the record companies took notice. They started issuing records by more "old-fashioned" artists such as Jimmie Rodgers (famous for the yodels he laced through his songs) and the Carter Family, or blues artists such as Bessie Smith. A.P. Carter and his wife Sara made up the Carter Family, along with Sara's cousin Maybelle, whose distinctive guitar picking—plucking the melody on the bass strings and an accompanying rhythm on the treble strings—influenced Woody throughout his life.

The Corncob Trio wasn't that good yet, but its members were enthusiastic and determined. They got a few gigs but usually ended up playing in the homes of their friends and family. One of Woody's favorite places was the Jennings household—a warm, intimate setting made all the more alluring by Matt's younger sister, Mary, a shy girl with a brilliant smile and smooth blond hair that fell past her shoulders. Mary was fifteen when Woody first began to notice her, and he was five years older.

At first they just smiled at one another across the room as the Corncob Trio practiced or played records on the phonograph. When there were other people around, Woody transformed from a fairly quiet, thoughtful young man into a clown—telling jokes or improvising hilarious mimes to the music. He was clearly different from the other fellows in Pampa, and Mary warmed to his difference. Soon they were holding hands, going to movies and spending as much time together as possible.

Romance bloomed in Charley's life as well—at least the hope of it. He had been feeling increasingly depressed and dejected since Nora's death, though his health had slowly improved. After several months he wrote to a lonely hearts club and was given the name of Miss Bettie Jean McPherson, with whom he began exchanging correspondence. In her letters Bettie Jean seemed chatty and energetic—a likeable woman. And because Charley missed having a home of his own, with a wife and children around him, it wasn't long before he invited Bettie Jean to travel to Pampa and marry him. She wasn't nearly as pretty as Nora, he discovered. In fact, she wasn't pretty at all. But the friendliness that had been apparent in her letters was just as evident in her personality. Charley married her the same day she arrived, and they moved into a tiny tourist "cottage"— more like a shack — on the edge of town.

Since the early days of their mail-order courtship, Charley had been under the impression that Bettie Jean was a licensed nurse. Shortly after their wedding, he learned that she was actually a self-taught "healer" and fortune-teller. He also discovered that she could be bossy and stubborn — even physically intimidating. Soon the cottage was crowded with her customers, and Charley began feeling neglected, not to mention disappointed. Things just weren't turning out the way he'd planned.

But Woody liked his stepmother. He'd been going to the local library to read books on a variety of subjects and, in the early 1930s, the occult was his favorite topic. He began dropping by Charley's cottage to discuss his theories on mental telepathy, extrasensory perception, astrology and dreams with Bettie Jean. He was so wrapped up in his experiments and readings that he didn't notice his father's gloominess or his younger sister's unhappiness. Because of Bettie Jean's controlling behavior, life for them was rapidly becoming unbearable. Charley avoided the house as much as possible, but Mary Jo had few options.

Woody was thinking of getting married himself, though he and Mary had been dating only a few months. He was just so happy lately. He had his music, his reading, his youth and his health. And he harbored a deep affection for the whole Jennings bunch. What could be more natural than marrying Mary and becoming a legal member of the family? Mary was a little surprised when Woody popped the question, and her father forbade the union. His daughter was still more of a child than a woman, and Woody wasn't the kind of husband he had imagined for her. But Woody wasn't about to give up. In the meantime, however, adventure beckoned.

Buried Treasure

or years the Guthries had talked about an astounding discovery Charley's father had made deep in Texas near the Mexican border. Jeremiah P. Guthrie had chiseled loose a few fragments of shiny rock during a trip to the region more than thirty years earlier, and had later determined that the rock was silver laced with gold, copper and other minerals! Or so he claimed. Jeremiah had marked the spot with a piece of paper and a stick and drawn several maps of the area. But in the years that followed, he never returned to unearth the riches that supposedly lay beneath the ground.

Jeremiah was dead now, but gossip about the silver mine still erupted from time to time. As his disappointment over his marriage deepened, Charley began to talk of nothing else. He was convinced that great wealth was his for the taking, provided he could find the site of the silver lode. He went on about it so much that he managed to convince his half-brother Jeff to join him on an expedition. When Woody got wind of the idea, he couldn't wait to hit the road. Roy had recently moved to Pampa, and he decided to tag along as well.

They loaded up Jeff's Model T truck with beans, gasoline, musical instruments and moonshine whiskey, and pulled out of Pampa in a festive mood. Woody rode in the back of the truck under a canvas tarp, where he could play his guitar freely. A cold winter wind was whipping across the panhandle when they started out, and dried balls of Russian thistle rolled across the road — tumbleweeds! To Woody, the real "boss" of the north Texas plains was the wind, since "there wasn't a high blade of anything up there to argue back." It whistled around the truck as the worn-out vehicle bounced along the highway on four bald tires. And it muffled the sounds of their voices so that they had to shout to hear each other. It roared behind them as they turned west onto Highway 66, which crossed the country from coast to coast, then south at Amarillo. And they still had five hundred miles to go!

When they reached Odessa — an oil-field town at the edge of the West Texas plains — the sprawling, twisted limbs of mesquite trees became visible, and the countryside began to change from grass-lands to more arid terrain. "I'd been used to looking out across the country on every side back up in the Panhandle and seeing the iron grass and more iron grass," Woody recalled. "Down here the mesquite rooted the iron grass out from the soil." They traveled for two days, taking turns at the wheel. On the second day, as they approached the desert, the landscape turned treeless again, becoming a vast expanse of dry, sandy earth. Low bushes hugged the ground, along with scattered bunches of stiff grass and several different types of cactus. Rocks of all sizes lay strewn across the terrain. In the far distance, high bluffs of rock were visible. These were the Chisos Mountains, surrounded — as Woody remembered — by "humpy yellow foothills in front and higher peaks and ridges beyond, rising up purplish and rose-colored against the sky."

They drove and drove, through tiny, dust-colored towns like Lajitas, Terlingua and Study Butte, and then into the mountains them-selves — mountains with names like "Hen Egg" and "Packsaddle." Finally they reached their destination, a ranch formerly owned by Woody's Uncle Gid Guthrie but now belonging to a man named Sam Nail. They were exhausted from their journey but jubilant and inspired. They had never seen a place as magical as this winding stretch of Texas. Sam Nail didn't think they'd find any silver or gold, but he offered them the use of an empty adobe hut nearby — just in case they were on to something. They unpacked their gear, then headed out into the desert seeking their fortune.

Jeremiah's old maps bore very little resemblance to the reality of the land, which was so vast and so brutal it could not possibly be fully explored in their lifetimes. The silver lode was supposed to lie near a spot where mineral waters spilled from the parched ground. But Sam Nail said these waters sprang up all over the desert — and vanished just as quickly. The Guthrie men soon real-ized their hunt was fruitless. But they stayed for a week anyway, joyous and free from the worries of work and home.

Woody marveled over the desert—a place of vast silences and relentless light. Power seemed to emanate from the earth itself, until sometimes the silence seemed deafening. Vultures circled through the sky, waiting for something to die. Brightly colored stones occasionally glittered in the sun. And along the river there were canyons and huge rock formations created by time itself. Whenever he encountered white-tailed deer or wild hogs, or discovered the tracks of mountain lions, he was amazed that any animals were able to survive—to thrive, even—in such a harsh environment. And in the evenings, as dusk approached, layers of color filled the sky: pinks and reds and lavenders more intense and startling than any sunset he had ever seen.

They went home at the end of the week, but the expedition had affected Woody deeply. In many ways, it had opened his eyes to the immensity of the world around him.

I'm Going
Where There's No Depression

s the 1930s dragged on, times got harder. All across the country people were suffering, especially in the Wheat Belt, which stretched a thousand miles from the Texas panhandle north to the Dakotas. A terrible drought had stricken the land, and the soil — once so productive — turned barren. Migrant workers had trouble finding jobs, and small farmers were losing their property. And the future looked just as bleak as the present.

In 1932, promising relief from the Great Depression, Franklin D. Roosevelt was elected president of the United States. The next year Congress passed legislation to spur business activity and ease unemployment. It also hoped to boost wages for the many laborers who earned less than $10 a week for the sixty hours or more they worked. The legislation recommended fewer hours and higher wages, but it did more for big business than it did for workers. And it had little effect in the Wheat Belt, where drought and unemployment were shattering the region's way of life.

Since the turn of the century, migrant workers had followed the wheat crop northward. By harvesting the grain from winter to spring and working in lumber or mining camps the rest of the year, they had always earned enough to survive — sometimes even enough to support a family, though most migrant workers were single men. Most of the time the migrants were welcomed by the farmers who employed them. They rode the rails for free (in boxcars), slept in the farmers' barns, ate at their tables, and were encouraged to spend their earnings in town after the harvest was over. Then they moved on.

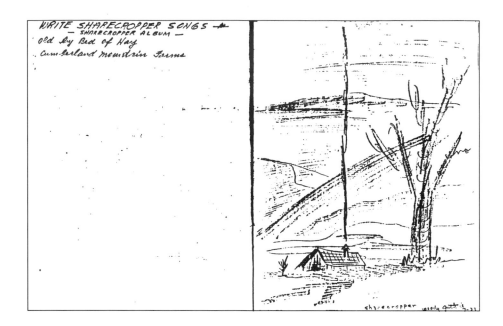

But when the United States entered World War I in 1917, life in the Wheat Belt changed dramatically. For one thing, the demand for wheat skyrocketed, and larger and larger tracts of land were converted to the crop. With so much acreage devoted to wheat, the need for workers shot up, too. Some migrants seized the opportunity to push for higher wages, and many joined unions such as the Agricultural Workers Industrial Union — one of the many unions affiliated with the Industrial Workers of the World, commonly known as "the Wobblies."

The farmers weren't happy about the unions and began pressuring local authorities to drive them out of town. Any tactic was fine with the farmers, as long as it got rid of the troublemakers. Union workers were pelted with rotten eggs, squirted with volleys of water, herded into holding pens, and even beaten. After World War I, tensions heightened even further as the demand for grain decreased and new waves of workers flooded the region. Then the Great Depression struck, and hard times spread to all types of farmers. The price of wheat and other crops plummeted, and small farmers were soon as bad off as the migrant workers. At one point, a bushel of corn was priced at less than nothing: It cost a farmer three cents just to "sell" it.

Before long, big companies began buying or leasing land in the region and using machines to till and harvest their crops. By

1933, more than 150,000 migrant jobs had been eliminated by the tractor-driven combine-harvester—a machine few small farmers could afford. With the drought, many small farmers found it impossible to survive at all. When the rains stopped coming, the earth simply began to blow away.

Pampa suffered like the rest of the country. The oil boom ended along with the rains. Farmers in the outlying areas began losing their crops—and eventually their lands, too. The ground turned from pale yellow and green to just plain brown. And the winds grew more destructive.

"The dust crawled down from the north and the banks pushed the farmers off their land," Woody wrote. "The big flat lakes dried away and left hollow places across the plains full of this hard, dry, crackled, gumbo mud. There isn't a healthier country than West Texas when it wants to be, but when the dust kept whistling down the line blacker and more of it, there was plenty of everything sick, and mad, and mean, and worried." Even music reflected the hard times. A Carter Family song called "No Depression" had the following chorus:

> *I'm going where there's no depression*
> *To the lovely land that's free from care*
> *I'll leave this world of toil and trouble*
> *My home's in heaven, I'm going there.*

In late October 1933, Woody and Mary married and moved into a small apartment above Jeff and Allene. They had finally won the half-hearted blessings of Mary's mother and survived from month to month on money Woody earned painting signs, working in the drugstore or playing music. Not long after the wedding, they took to the road with Jeff and Allene as part of a traveling show organized and paid for by a rancher named Claude Taylor. The group spent several months at the Taylor ranch planning and perfecting their act, a rejuvenating period for everyone involved and an unexpected honeymoon for Woody and Mary. For the show itself, Jeff played the fiddle and performed magic tricks, while Allene backed him up on the accordion. Woody dressed up like a ragged farmer and clowned around on stage. But the show didn't make much money, and Taylor soon called it quits.

Back in Pampa, Woody began putting together a songbook of sorts, which he playfully called *Alonzo M. Zilch's Own Collection of Original Songs and Ballads.* It contained traditional songs and a few original compositions — which consisted of Woody's lyrics set to the melodies of popular tunes. He was still reading voraciously at the local library, mostly books on the occult, and comparing notes with his stepmother. Soon "customers" began knocking on his door seeking advice. Woody listened carefully to their complaints and wishes, then advised them on the future. He never charged them any money for his services, unlike Bettie Jean, his mentor. Nor did he notice that she was becoming increasingly cruel toward his father and Mary Jo. Woody was wrapped up in his own passions, which seemed to encompass just about everything, including the construction of adobe houses.

Mary marveled at the range of her husband's interests, worried over several of them — like his experiments in mental telepathy — but was more concerned with other things. In the spring of 1935, about the same time she discovered she was pregnant, the sky went crazy.

CHAPTER 9

Dust Pneumonia

est Texans were used to dust storms. The panhandle had long been subject to cycles of rain and drought, so it wasn't unusual to see the wind kicking up small twisters of sandy-colored dirt or to feel the subtle sting of grit in the air. Dust storms visited towns throughout the Great Plains region, Woody recalled. But they were the "blackest and the thickest" along the Texas panhandle. "Just go to Amarillo, Texas, and...within walking distance 'round there you'll find you a good dust storm to deal with," he said.

No one knew how long this drought would last. Church congregations prayed for showers, and the town folks analyzed the sky for signs of a good storm, but the dryness held and the dust grew thicker. It penetrated the cracks and crevices of the ramshackle buildings and drizzled across the furniture and dishes. When the wind blew, dust stung the skin and clotted the vision. Because the air was perpetually charged with dirt, people fell victim to a variety of respiratory ailments and began calling them all "dust pneumonia." Most of the time, they joked about it. There wasn't much else they could do. "I've got Texas in my heart, but Oklahoma in my lungs," they'd laugh. But deep down, they grew afraid.

On April 14, 1935, in the middle of the afternoon, the townsfolk noticed the sky darkening over the horizon, as though a tremendous rainstorm were approaching. As they continued to gaze into the distance, however, they realized the black clouds held dust, not rain! As far as they could see, the clouds boiled and boomed, with birds thronging ahead of them, desperate for escape. The temperature began to drop, and the sky grew as dim as dusk, then dark as nightfall. It was a terrifying sight, worse than anything they could have imagined.

"Just to see a thing of that kind a comin' towards you, you wouldn't know exactly what it was," Woody later explained, "'cause it's a freak-looking thing. You never saw anything like it before."

It was a Sunday, he recalled. "A whole bunch of us was standin' just outside of this little town....And so we watched the dust storm come up like the Red Sea closin' in on the Israel children." The people rushed for their houses and storm cellars — if they had them. They shut all their doors and windows, sealing the cracks with towels and old rags, and waited together for what many thought was the end of the world.

"It got so dark you couldn't see your hand before your face," Woody remembered. "You couldn't see anybody in the room." A light bulb "looked just about like a cigarette a burnin'. And that was all the light that you could get out of it."

The clouds swirled with the dark topsoil and clayey earth of the northern Great Plains — hundreds of thousands of tons of it, from as far away as North Dakota. The storm had been traveling toward them for many hours, gaining density and speed as it advanced. By the time it hit Pampa, the wind was gusting at velocities of up to seventy miles an hour, battering the walls and rattling the windows.

Woody and Mary and several other people who had crowded into their shack sat in the cramped living room and waited, most with wet cloths over their mouths to filter out the dust. As they huddled together, listening to the winds and the dirt pounding their little town, they began to discuss their fate. Would the storm ever end? Or would it destroy everything in its path, including the people of Pampa?

"They just said, 'Well, this is the end. This is the end of the world.'" Woody recalled. "Even the old timers that lived there for fifty years said they never seen anything like it."

Eventually the wall of dust did pass, though the winds raged throughout the night, creating drifts so deep they resembled snow — black snow. By the time the storm ended completely, it had battered the Oklahoma and Texas panhandles along with parts of Kansas, Colorado and New Mexico. It made a lasting impression on Woody. He even wrote a song about it a few years later called "Dust Storm Disaster." From the first verse, the lines were simple, vivid:

On the fourteenth day of April, of 1935,
There struck the worst of dust storms that ever filled the sky.
You could see that dust storm coming,
The cloud looked death-like black.
And through our mighty nation, it left a dreadful track.

The day after the storm, in an article describing the catastrophe, a reporter visiting the region called the storm-ravaged areas a "Dust Bowl." The name was fitting.

At first the townsfolk were excited to be alive, to have survived the devastation of what came to be known as the Great Dust Storm. But after a few days their spirits began to sink. What was happening to the land that had always supported them? The ground refused to yield any crops. The banks refused to loan them money. Their farms were foreclosed and their personal belongings auctioned out from under them to pay their debts — and still they owed. And who knew how long these hard times would last? It seemed a lifetime since any substantial rains had fallen.

For some months — even before the big storm — folks had been packing up their few belongings and leaving town, not just in the Texas panhandle where Woody lived, but in Oklahoma, Kansas, Nebraska, Missouri, Arkansas, Iowa, Colorado and South Dakota — farm states, for the most part. Most of these migrants headed west, and most made the trek by car: Battered wrecks stuffed with families, food and a few odds and ends. They were bound for California, where the valleys were lush and the work plentiful — or so they had heard. They hoped to make a new life, to find a little piece of land and start over.

Woody noticed these travelers and wondered about them. He saw the line of jalopies south of town along Highway 66, with flimsy crates and spare tires tied to the roofs and bumpers. Some journeyed on foot, hitching rides when they could. A few straggled into town for gas or provisions. They looked prematurely old, their faces lined and leathery from the wind, their bodies bent from hard labor and disappointment.

Woody had heard rumors about the good life California promised. But for the time being, he was too wrapped up in his music and impending fatherhood to wonder too hard about that distant place.

CHAPTER 10

Highway 66

oody spent money as fast as he earned it, sometimes faster — either that or he gave it away, much to Mary's dismay. In fact, Woody's attitude toward money upset most of the people closest to him, who thought he should be making a real living with a full-time job, especially now that he was married with a baby on the way. Money *was* important to Woody. It was just that he despised it! Oh, he'd admit, it did come in handy sometimes. But it also destroyed folks — like his own family, for instance. If his father hadn't been so preoccupied with making money, he might have been around to prevent Clara's fire or Nora's illness — at least that's how Woody saw it. So he promised himself to focus on the important things in life. He was still in the process of discovering exactly what those things were, but he knew one of them was music.

In the fall of 1935, Mary gave birth to a daughter. They named her Gwendolyn Gail but called her "Teeny." Woody marveled over this fragile new life, over her tuft of blond hair, her miniature fingers and toes. Sometimes he sang quiet lullabies to her, and often he bragged about her, but he left the burden of her care to Mary. He began staying out late, sometimes not coming home at all. When he did show up, he passed his time arguing with Mary or sleeping. He was fully aware of his responsibilities as a father, and he rebelled against them, partly because he'd made his own rules for so long, and partly because he was afraid. His daughter seemed so magical, so vulnerable. He was terrified of failing her — so terrified he avoided fatherhood as much as possible. If he had stopped to think about it, he might have spotted the holes in his logic. But as most of his friends and family had already discovered, Woody rarely stopped to think about his choices.

Fatherhood wasn't easy in the 1930s. Even men who wanted to work found it difficult to earn a living. In Pampa, with the oil boom over and the drought hanging on, the number of available jobs continued to shrink. The situation was just about as bad in big industrial cities like Chicago. Factory jobs had dried up, and bills mounted. Families who couldn't pay their debts had their furniture and other belongings repossessed. Many were evicted from their homes, their few remaining possessions piled on the sidewalks. Men were expected to be tough, to guide their families through hard times. But as the Depression deepened, many found it difficult to stand by and watch their children go without. It was just too painful to bear.

It wasn't easy for the women, either, being pregnant when there was little food to eat, or running a household on meager — often nonexistent — budgets. But they were resourceful: When the cupboard held only an onion and a bit of potato, they created soup for a family of five. They patched and re-patched their family's clothes, made underwear out of empty flour sacks, went without food so the children could eat, and often looked after relatives who were worse-off than they were.

Woody and Mary were luckier than many folks. From the time they were married until shortly after Teeny's birth, their families lived nearby and tried to help out when they could. But when his marriage to Bettie Jean ended, Charley moved to Arkansas to start over again, and the Jennings family began to grow impatient with their son-in-law. Woody could feel their resentment mounting, and he turned to music for refuge.

"I made up new words to old tunes and sung them everywhere I'd go," he wrote. "Some people liked me, hated me, walked with me, walked over me, jeered me, cheered me, rooted me and hooted me....But I decided that songs was a music and a language of all tongues." It brought people together, even people facing devastating losses. For a few hours at a country dance or in a saloon, music could ease a person's troubled mind. Soon Woody was writing verses about the drought, about the long road to California, and all the other images crowding his mind.

"At first it was funny songs of what all's wrong, and how it turned out good or bad," he explained. "Then I got a little braver and made up songs telling what I thought was wrong and how to make it right, songs that said what everybody in that country was thinking."

A number of his early songs described the Great Dust Storm or dust in general. Though he usually borrowed melodies from traditional tunes or hymns, he had a natural flair for writing lyrics. His words were biting and sarcastic, defiant, determined, humorous or corny — often all of these things. But the words were always simple, never pretentious. In "Dusty Old Dust" he painted a clear picture:

> *A dust storm hit, and it hit like thunder;*
> *It dusted us over and it covered us under;*
> *Blocked out the traffic and blocked out the sun.*
> *Straight for home all the people did run.*

And through all the verses he weaved a plaintive chorus, which sounded even more mournful when he sang it in his unadorned, slightly nasal voice:

> *So long, it's been good to know you;*
> *So long, it's been good to know you;*
> *So long, it's been good to know you,*
> *This dusty old dust is a gettin' my home,*
> *And I've got to be driftin' along.*

The stream of migrants continued along Highway 66, and Woody grew restless. He felt bored in Pampa. He knew everybody in town, all the stories, all the songs. Most people were struggling, and he couldn't help wondering for what. The town's future seemed as bleak as the colorless fields, as fruitless as the earth. There was nothing left for him to learn there. If he continued to hang around, Woody feared, he might grow soft and useless, or dry up and blow away with everything else.

"I remember a frog they found in Okemah, once when they tore the old bank building down," he wrote. "He'd been sealed up in solid concrete for thirty-two years, and had almost turned to jelly. Jelly. Blubbery. Soft and oozy. Slicky and wiggly. I [didn't] want to turn to no jelly....I [wanted] more than anything else for

Family on the road, Midwest, c. 1938 (Copyright the Dorothea Lange Collection, The Oakland Museum, The City of Oakland. Gift of Paul S. Taylor).

my belly to stay hard and stay wound up tight and stay alive."

As 1936 rolled on, as empty and unpromising as the years before it, the road began to beckon Woody. He began taking short trips out of town: first to East Texas, where Tom and Nonie Moore had settled, then to Oklahoma and Arkansas to visit Roy and Charley. It was as though he were rehearsing for the big journey, the one thousands had already made and thousands more were making still. Before the year was out, with little more than a guitar and a bundle of paintbrushes, he walked the long mile from Pampa to Highway 66 and started drifting west.

CHAPTER 11

Little Red Songbook

oody had planned on hitchhiking, but rides were hard to come by. For one thing, with so many people walking down the road, he had a lot of competition. But he made the short trip into New Mexico, where he picked up a little money painting signs. Then he tried hitching again, but soon decided he'd make better progress "riding the rails."

The days of free boxcar travel for migrant workers had passed. Hopping freight trains was now strictly illegal, and getting caught could win a person a jail sentence or a beating. But it was still the primary form of transportation for single men, most of them migrant workers — sometimes called "hobos" — who had no other resources. They'd jump on board as the trains pulled out of the railroad yards, and they'd keep out of sight until they reached their destination. Sometimes the boxcars Woody rode were crammed with men, many of them drunk or half-crazed from hunger and lack of sleep. Brawls were commonplace, and so was racism — usually on the part of whites, many of whom refused to share space with black travelers.

As the trains pulled into stations along the way, the men would hop off and scrounge around for food and money for booze and tobacco. Quite a few hobos knocked on doors asking for hand-outs, but Woody was "too proud" for such behavior. If he couldn't earn money from his painting or guitar playing, he'd usually go without. When he did have cash, though, he shared it with his fellow travelers — or gave it away completely.

Sometimes, to escape the railroad guards' notice, the men rode on top of the boxcars, with no protection from the wind and rain, or hung between them, desperately clutching the ladders or slick steel bars. It was an exhausting journey. But when the train rolled into California, Woody quickly forgot the hardships. The place was simply gorgeous, as magnificent and fertile as all the stories had claimed.

"The world turned into such a thick green garden of fruits and vegetables that I didn't know if I was dreaming or not," he wrote. Compared to the drabness of the Dust Bowl, the colors and fragrances were startling. Sumptuous fruits seemed to blossom from every tree, and Woody immediately understood why so many fantastic tales had been told about the place. "All you have got to do out in this country," one of the stories boasted, "is to just pour water around some roots and yell, 'Grapes!' and next morning the leaves are full grown, and the grapes are hanging in big bunches, all nice and ready to pick!"

But there was another side to California — a side Woody had not anticipated at all. The authorities had begun monitoring all entry points along the border. When they spotted people who looked as though they might be migrants from the Dust Bowl or farm belt, they intercepted them. "They asked us questions when we come across the line," Woody recalled. "Asked us where we's from and all about it. And then they tried to turn a lot of us back — the hobos, the boys that was riding the freight trains and hitchhiking down the road that didn't have any money in their pockets." There were families turned back, too, most of them traveling in beat-up cars. They'd be asked to show the police just how much money they were carrying. If it wasn't enough, they were refused entry.

Life wasn't much easier for those who did make it into the state. Back home they'd been given handbills advertising plentiful work gathering fruit in California, but when they arrived they found just the opposite. There were hundreds of thousands of people wanting jobs — and little work available. In some places the fruit lay rotting in heaps on the ground, while migrants camped down the road, lacking food and employment.

"I seen things out there that I wouldn't believe," Woody recalled. "Hundreds and hundreds and hundreds and hundreds and thousands of families of people livin' around under railroad bridges" and "in old rusty beat-up houses that they'd made out of tow sacks and old dirty rags and corrugated iron that they got out of the dumps....And a lot of times I've seen three or four hundred families of people tryin' to get along on a stream of water that wasn't any bigger than the stream of water that comes from your faucet when you go into the kitchen and turn the faucet on."

There was another disturbing element, too. Many native Californians despised the newcomers. In the decades preceding the Great Depression, most migrant workers in California had been single men — most of them Mexican nationals. Because they were rooted in another country and unfamiliar with the American legal system, these workers usually appeared with the harvests and then vanished again — like the migrant workers in the Wheat Belt. But now the state was filling up with whole families of poor whites, and the locals were afraid these newcomers would settle down and apply for government relief when they failed to find jobs. They began calling them all "Okies," whether they had come from Oklahoma or not. The way they pronounced the word, it sounded like the nastiest of insults.

Woody visited his Aunt Laura and cousin Amalee in the town of Turlock for several weeks, then headed back home to Mary and little Gwen. Along the way, lacking money for rooms, he slept under bridges or in hobo camps, where he listened to the men discuss their hard times. Many of them were Wobblies who spoke angrily of the way they'd been treated and what they intended to do about it. They hoped to organize the entire American work force into "one big union" and, eventually, take over the various industries from the rich men — the capitalists — who owned them. After all, they argued, wasn't it their hard labor that had made these men their millions? Why should the workers get paid so little when they did all the work? The Wobblies preferred direct action to political action. They were more likely to sabotage factory lines and call work stoppages to further their ends. It was quicker and more effective than voting. They published their own newspapers and even compiled a songbook called, simply enough, "the little red songbook," a collection of political ballads and marches and parodies of hymns.

Many of these songs had been written by a man called Joe Hill, a Swedish citizen (born under the name Joel Haaglund) who had served briefly as a Wobbly organizer until his execution in Utah in 1915. Hill had been convicted of shooting a Salt Lake City storekeeper and son, but the conviction was based on circumstantial evidence. Though none of the witnesses could identify him as the gunman, public sentiment in Salt Lake City ran strongly against him, thanks in large part to the local newspapers, which published numerous articles vilifying him and criticizing his Wobbly affiliations. Hill's prosecution and execution stirred public interest nationwide. Even Woodrow Wilson, then president of the United States, pleaded for clemency on his behalf. After Hill's execution, thirty thousand people marched in protest in Chicago, and Wobblies everywhere began calling him a martyr.

Twenty years had passed by the time Woody picked up a copy of the little red songbook, but he was immediately intrigued by Hill's lyrics. They were direct, simple and articulated the poor workers' feelings of frustration, anger and determination. One of Hill's finest creations was a song called "The Preacher and the Slave," set to the tune of an old gospel hymn but with new lyrics that criticized Americans for trivializing the plight of the poor:

> *Long-haired preachers come out every night,*
> *Try to tell you what's wrong and what's right;*
> *But when asked how 'bout something to eat*
> *They will answer with voices so sweet:*

> *You will eat, bye and bye,*
> *In that glorious land above the sky;*
> *Work and pray, live on hay,*
> *You'll get pie in the sky when you die.*

Since Woody had recently begun writing songs about social conditions himself, he was fascinated by Hill's approach. None of Hill's songs were written to evoke sympathy, nor did they advocate the passive acceptance of defeat. Rather, they used humor and satire to encourage the poor to take responsibility for their plight.

Woody traveled back and forth between Texas, California and other points in the west several times in 1936 and 1937, riding the freights or hitchhiking, as on his first journey. Mary stayed behind in Pampa in the tiny, dusty shack, doing her best to raise a toddler on very little money. Sometimes Woody sent her cash in the mail, but usually he didn't. In late 1936, when Mary discovered

Tractored out, Childress County, Texas, 1938 (Copyright the Dorothea Lange Collection, The Oakland Museum, The City of Oakland. Gift of Paul S. Taylor).

she was pregnant again, Woody said he was happy about it, but soon headed back to California.

His political beliefs were changing rapidly. In Pampa, before his first trip west, he'd been aware of the farmers' plight and concerned about the hard times, but his life had centered on other things — music mostly, and psychology, and his love for Mary. Now as he traveled the highways and saw the flood of migrants heading west, the hard times began to affect him deeply. The blind optimism and bravery of these families inspired him and horrified him at the same time — for he knew the dreary future that lay ahead of them in the so-called promised land. But he also understood the difficult choice they had made. He knew the travelers were thinking about their last days at home, remembering "the old tractor setting back down there covered up with dust, the cow standin' up on top of the barn and lookin' out across that dead sea of dust." As bad as conditions in California were, he knew the migrants would rather have a hope for the future — even the slightest of hopes — than to be trapped on a farm so deep in debt they'd never get out again.

Lefty Lou

oody's Aunt Laura moved from Turlock to Los Angeles, and in the spring of 1937, Woody headed there, too. There were quite a few members of the Guthrie clan living in Los Angeles at the time. Woody was simply the latest newcomer and soon began tagging along with one of his cousins, Jack Guthrie.

They made an interesting pair. Though they were about the same age, Jack was tall and good-looking, with a polished singing voice and a burning desire to be a cowboy in a movie. Woody was shorter than average and slight in build. He never worried too much about his appearance, so his clothes were always rumpled-looking and loose. While Jack was an accomplished musician, Woody was merely average. Yet he possessed a certain kind of spirit — an intensity and sincerity — that endeared him to people whenever he performed.

Jack called himself "Oklahoma" for show-biz purposes and soon began taking Woody along on auditions and gigs. He also introduced him to Roy and Georgia Crissman, who had come to Los Angeles from Missouri in the early 1930s. Maxine, the eldest of the Crissmans' two daughters, was just a few years younger than Woody, yet she and Woody didn't seem to have much in common. Maxine was serious and well-dressed, and Woody seemed a little goofy. But when they began to sing together, the result was startling. Their voices blended into a perfect harmony, with Woody taking the high part to Maxine's strong alto. They even liked the same types of songs: old hymns and country ballads.

Maxine was a "tall, thin-faced, corn-fed Missouri farm girl with a voice rough and husky," Woody later wrote. "Lefty Lou," he called her. Soon they were singing together whenever they could spare the time and spending long hours talking about life. But the relationship was strictly friendship, based on mutual respect and admiration — and probably a fair dose of loneliness on Woody's part. Romance wasn't part of the picture. Woody was married with a family, after all, though that hadn't stopped him from pursuing other women in his travels.

In July, Mary gave birth to a second daughter and named her Sue. She sent word to Woody, hoping he'd at least come for a visit, but he stayed in Los Angeles and continued to perform with Jack. Most of the time, Jack did all the singing and serious guitar playing, while Woody filled in with harmonica riffs or simple chords on the guitar. He didn't mind. It was all an adventure, as far as he was concerned.

That summer Jack arranged for them to have a regular morning spot on radio station KFVD, which broadcast out of Los Angeles. They weren't paid for their services, but they were thrilled at the opportunity anyway. They christened their segment "The Oklahoma and Woody Show," presenting a collection of cowboy songs — few of them *real* cowboy songs, mostly Hollywood creations from the movies. Not surprisingly, given their previous experience, there was more Oklahoma than Woody drifting over the airwaves. But the show was popular. Several hundred fan letters arrived the first few weeks it was on the air. In late August, J. Frank Burke, the station owner, gave them a second half-hour slot at eleven o'clock each night.

Sometimes Woody brought Maxine down to the station to accompany him over the air. When autumn rolled around and Jack decided he wanted out of the show (he had a family to support and needed money), Maxine stepped in to take his place. Woody even wrote a theme song for the new program, which began with the following verse:

> *Drop whatever you are doing,*
> *Stop your work and worry, too;*
> *Sit right down and take it easy,*
> *Here comes Woody and Lefty Lou.*

From the start, they were a hit. They got rid of the cowboy songs and started performing the music they loved. During his months on the road, riding the rails and sleeping in hobo camps, Woody had developed a large repertoire of traditional tunes, country ballads and hymns, picked up from migrants on the road — most of them displaced farmers from the Wheat Belt and midwestern states. Now he began singing these songs over the air and talking about his travels: the sights he had seen and the hard times people faced. Letters flooded the KFVD offices. People were listening — his people were listening. And they considered Woody and Maxine kindred spirits, and they wanted more.

Sometimes the radio signal traveled several states away, as far away as Pampa, where Mary listened proudly with her two small daughters. From time to time, Woody dedicated songs to her. He had promised to bring her to California as soon as he got the money together. Now that he was a big success on the radio, Mary expected to be packing her bags very soon. In November, with fan mail arriving in ever-increasing amounts, Frank Burke added a third slot for the show — at noon each day — and offered Woody and Maxine $20 a week, minimum pay, complete with a contract. Soon after signing it, Woody summoned Mary to Los Angeles.

Since his own arrival that spring, Woody had been camping out in various people's houses, most often his Aunt Laura's, so he and Mary set up housekeeping there. Mary — barely twenty years old — was overwhelmed by the change. Not only was California vastly different from drought-ridden Pampa, but Woody was different, too. He was deeply involved in his music, writing his own songs and preparing for each day's shows, and always running from one place to another. He also seemed distant. Mary suspected there were other women involved but had no idea what to do about them. She and Woody began to quarrel.

Woody was more accustomed to independence than marriage. And the presence of two small children, still so helpless and needy, left him feeling trapped. So it wasn't long before he reverted to old patterns — disappearing often and offering no explanation upon his return. In December, Mary's brother Matt arrived. Even Jeff and Allene had relocated from Pampa, hoping to make it big in radio, as Woody had. The presence of close relatives, particularly Matt, helped ease the tensions between Woody and Mary, but it added tensions, too. Several of Woody's relatives expected to be invited on his show and, for the most part, Woody was happy to oblige them. But the show became too chaotic when they appeared, and listeners began complaining about the change. Frank Burke agreed with the listeners and told Woody to stick to Lefty Lou.

In early 1938, Woody got an offer that appeared to solve his problems. Radio station XELO, just over the border in Tijuana, Mexico, wanted Woody and Maxine to anchor a music show there. The station had a powerful signal. Most of its broadcasts reached U.S. audiences. XELO not only offered Woody and Maxine more money, but asked them to line up a group of other musicians as well. The new show would feature a variety of entertainers, with Woody and Maxine as the regular hosts. Although he was still bound by contract to KFVD, Woody jumped at the opportunity, and the gang packed up and moved to Mexico.

But the XELO arrangement was little short of disaster. Woody began drinking heavily at local bars. By show time each day, he was muddled and hard to control. With a growing cast of family members all eager to perform — and no one to direct them — the broadcasts became increasingly unruly. After a few weeks the checks stopped coming, and the show soon ended completely. Woody and the others trailed back to Los Angeles.

Frank Burke, the owner of KFVD, was an unusual man. He hadn't complained when Woody broke his contract and ran off to Mexico. And now that Woody was back and wanting his old show, Burke was happy to give it to him — except for the eleven p.m. slot, which had been filled by somebody else. As far as bosses went, Burke was pretty easygoing, happiest when he was on the air himself, talking about politics. He was furious over what was happening in the state, the way the migrants were being herded into crowded, unsanitary camps and paid next to nothing for their labor — if they were lucky enough to find work at all. Sometimes big trucks would pull into the camps to recruit workers for the day or for the week, but they left with only a small fraction of those clamoring for employment. Many of the camps were run by the big fruit growers themselves, who charged the migrants rent and forced them to buy all their provisions at the camp store, where prices were high. The migrant workers watched their wages dwindle away as quickly as they earned them, and the families could never seem to get ahead of the game. Woody was concerned about the situation himself. Most of his listeners were recent migrants, many of them from the Dust Bowl region.

"All the newspaper headlines was full of stuff about Dust Bowl refugees," he said. "Refugees here, refugees yonder, refugees everwhere that you looked." It was easier for the natives to look down on the migrants if they were called refugees. But Woody knew them as real people—proud, industrious folks who had come to California because they wanted to work. They weren't looking for charity any more than the natives were looking to give it.

"All these people didn't go out there to loaf around," Woody explained. "They didn't go out there to have a good time. They went out there for one reason, and absolutely one reason, and that was because they thought that they could get some work.... They called [them] Dust Bowl refugees, but then there's more than one kind of a refugee. There's refugees that take refuge under railroad bridges and there's refugees that take refuge in public office."

Woody was happy to express his opinions over the air, and his listeners seemed to appreciate it. When he began to exhaust his repertoire of songs, he tried performing a few of his own compositions—and the listeners liked them, too. Some were funny, like "Talking Dust Bowl," which described the plight of the average refugee:

> *Rain quit and the wind got high,*
> *And a black old dust storm filled the sky,*
> *And I swapped my farm for a Ford machine,*
> *And I poured it full of this gasoline,*
> *And I started— rocking and a-rolling—*
> *Over the mountains out towards the old peach bowl.*

Woody didn't sing this song, but spoke the words in a rhythmical tone while strumming a few simple chords on his guitar. By the end of the song, his car wrecked and the family broke, he tells how

> *I bummed up a spud or two,*
> *And my wife fixed up a 'tater stew.*
> *We poured the kids full of it. Mighty thin stew, though.*
> *You could read a magazine right through it.*

...if it had been just a little bit thinner,
Some of these here politicians could have seen through it.

Other songs, such as "Do Re Mi"— a euphemism for "cash money"—
satirized actual events:

Lots of folks back east, they say,
Leavin' home ev'ry day,
Beatin' the hot old dusty way
To the California line.
Cross the desert sands they roll,
Getting out of that old dust bowl.
They think they're goin' to a sugar bowl,
But here is what they find.
Now the police at the port of entry say,
"You're number fourteen thousand for today."

Oh, if you ain't got the do re mi, folks,
If you ain't got the do re mi,
Why, you better go back to beautiful Texas,
Oklahoma, Kansas, Georgia, Tennessee.
California is a garden of Eden,
A paradise to live in or see.
But believe it or not,
You won't find it so hot,
If you ain't got the do re mi.

In the late spring of 1938, Woody and Mary moved into their own
apartment. Woody's younger brother George, who had recently
arrived, moved with them. But the transition only heightened tensions between husband and wife, and the quarrels grew worse
than ever.

By June, both Woody and Maxine were tired. Keeping up with
the daily shows had become grueling work. Woody was growing
restless, eager to hit the road again. And Maxine had developed
anemia. They asked Burke if they could take a break and—

amenable as always—he agreed. Since Woody wanted to travel, Burke asked him to investigate conditions in the migrant camps. There were rumors afloat that labor organizers were being brutalized and jailed. The California governorship was up for grabs, and Burke supported a candidate named Culbert Olsen. If what Burke had been hearing was true, then Olsen would want to know about it. And Woody was eager for the job assignment.

CHAPTER 1 3

A New Deal

he country was still in terrible economic shape. More than one fourth of the labor force was unemployed, and small landowners continued to be displaced. Although Roosevelt had convinced Congress to pass legislation boosting economic activity in different sectors of the nation, the results had been erratic. The Agricultural Adjustment Administration — established to help farmers — benefitted large landholders but did nothing at all for the three million tenant farmers who owned no land at all. Before it was declared unconstitutional in 1935, the National Recovery Administration established the right of workers to join unions to press for better working conditions and higher pay. But most unions excluded African Americans, women and unskilled laborers. And more than ten million workers had no jobs at all. The Works Progress Administration provided some employment on projects such as bridges and dams — even jobs as simple as raking leaves. The WPA also hired artists, writers and actors for a variety of assignments, from documenting life among the rural poor to staging performances for working-class folks. Government intervention did foster a sense of hope in the country — more hope than before — but there was still enormous suffering, particularly among blacks and migrant workers. These groups were largely unaffected by the many reforms that comprised Roosevelt's "New Deal," and they remained outside the public consciousness despite the support of Eleanor Roosevelt, the first lady.

People wanted relief. Most depressions lasted two or three years before conditions improved. But this one had stretched on for almost a decade with no end in sight. The poor of the nation seethed. They had nothing. How long did the government and the big companies and the banks think they'd stand for it?

In Wisconsin, his land auctioned out from under him by the bank, an angry farmer fended off authorities for more than three months, refusing to leave his property. In Arkansas, five hundred farmers marched into town with guns and demanded food for their families. In Chicago and New York, when families were evicted, local unemployment councils helped carry their furniture back into their apartments. In Iowa, a group of farmers tarred and feathered a judge who had okayed numerous land foreclosures. Even workers who had jobs were angry. They were required to work at a brutal pace for low wages. When they missed work, they ran the risk of being fired — even if they were sick. And when they were laid off, they had nothing to fall back on. Workers who had devoted ten or twenty years to the company could be cut from the payroll without warning or severance pay.

For these workers, unions seemed to offer the best hope, though there were limitations to their effectiveness. Most fell under the umbrella of the American Federation of Labor, which had been organizing workers by their various skills, or crafts, since the late 19th century. But the AFL failed to reach out to the unskilled labor force, which included migrant workers, miners, dock workers and others. Only when the Wobblies came along in 1905 and the American Communist party sprang up in 1919 did any organizers aim their efforts at unskilled workers. And it wasn't until 1938, when John L. Lewis formed the Congress of Industrial Organizations — with the support of the Communists — that workers began to be unionized by entire industries, such as autoworkers, instead of by their individual skills, such as welding. Communists were also instrumental in getting Congress to approve unemployment insurance and Social Security benefits. And when Woody began visiting the migrant camps in California, the Communists were on the scene organizing the workers. At the time, they were virtually the only group actively involved in easing the migrants' plight.

Woody was stunned by conditions in the camps — hundreds of families jammed into tight, unsanitary spaces. Many lived out of their cars, traveling from place to place with all their belongings strapped on tight, obvious targets for the "labor contractors" paid to round up workers at rock-bottom wages. Other families built shelters for themselves out of discarded objects. Their ingenuity was remarkable — and poignant.

"About every few feet [in a typical camp]...you'd walk past a shack just sort of made out of everything in general," Woody remembered, "— old strips of asphalt tar paper, double gunny sacks, an old dress, shirt, pair of overhalls, stretched up to cover half a side of a wall; bumpy corrugated iron, cement sacks, orange and apple crates took apart and nailed together with old rusty burnt nails from the cinder piles. Through a little square window on the side of a house, [you'd] hear bedsprings creaking and people talking. Men played cards, whittled, and women talked about work they'd struck and work they were hunting for. Dirt was on the floor of the house, and all kinds and colors of crawling and flying bugs come and went like they were getting paid for it."

Money was so hard to come by that entire families worked in the fields, picking cotton or fruit, when they could get a job. Children were literally starving to death, or working themselves to death, or both. A film crew documenting life in one of the camps captured a heartbreaking scene: A young girl, probably no older than twelve or thirteen, lay sleeping on a burlap sack on the ground, her hands picking invisible peas from the air.

Woody was surprised at the welcome he received in these camps. Many of the migrants had listened regularly to his KFVD broadcasts, and when they realized who he was they greeted him warmly. Woody would stay and talk a while, then pull out his guitar and start a song. Soon families would gather around him, calling out the names of tunes for him to play, often crying when he played them, their longing for home intensified.

These people were at the mercy of an agricultural system far bigger — and even more cold-blooded — than the one that had driven them from their homes. Millions of acres of California land were concentrated in the hands of a few hundred growers. The most powerful were members of Associated Farmers, which was something like a union — only a union for bosses, not workers. And unlike labor unions, which strove to equalize the distribution of wealth and humanize working conditions, Associated Farmers focused on accumulating as much of the profits as possible for its members, at the expense of the migrants who did the work. When Congress approved a series of payments through the Agricultural Adjustment Administration — an initiative intended to bring relief to struggling farmers — most of the money flowed into the hands of the big property owners, many of them members of Associated Farmers. In California, for example, in the cotton industry, the richest two and a half percent of the growers received thirty-three percent of the AAA payments.

These landholders stood to gain from the migrants' misery. The less money they paid the workers to pick fruit or cotton, the more profits they could shore up themselves. When the migrants began to organize to combat the low wages, the landholders hired local thugs, called "vigilantes," to bust them up and drive the organizers out of the region. Members of the local police forces often participated in the attacks. Workers and organizers were brutally beaten, even murdered, and migrant families lived in terror.

The fact that it was the *Communists* organizing the migrants incensed the growers even more. Since their party's founding in 1919, the Communists had been viewed as the most militant of the radical groups. After all, Communists had actually overthrown the Russian government in 1917! When the American Communist party began drawing members, most of them from the working class, many people were convinced they were out to overthrow the U.S. government, too, and the Communists themselves did little to soften their image.

But in the late 1930s, they eased their stance somewhat and started working with other groups to organize unskilled workers and combat fascism, which was escalating in Europe under the leadership of Adolf Hitler. Since President Roosevelt supported labor unions, the Communists supported many of his programs. Even so, they continued to arouse fear and scorn among many American citizens.

***

Shortly after Woody began touring the camps, Maxine fell in love and decided to end her radio career permanently. Woody returned to the airwaves after his hiatus, traveling back and forth between Los Angeles and the little towns and camps dotting California's central valley. With Maxine gone, the show was changing in several ways. Before, Woody had concentrated on singing country songs and telling funny stories, but now he began to discuss his rapidly evolving political ideas over the air. His experiences also influenced his song writing. He began to stray further from his country repertoire, writing lyrics that reflected conditions in the "Hoovervilles," as the camps were known. In the summer of

Oklahoma drought refugees, 1935
(Copyright the Dorothea Lange Collection, The Oakland Museum,
The City of Oakland. Gift of Paul S. Taylor).

1938, he wrote one of his most moving songs, taking the melody from an old hymn the Carter Family often performed called "This World Is Not My Home." The original hymn had a tone of resignation and offered little hope for a better life in this world. Like the long-haired preachers Joe Hill had parodied, the hymn looked toward the heavens for relief, where "treasures are laid up somewhere beyond the blue." Woody's lyrics transformed the piece, lending it a keen edge of anger, yet there was more to the song than simple rage. Woody's words witnessed the suffering of hundreds of thousands of actual people and underscored the utter senselessness of their plight. He called it "I Ain't Got No Home":

> *I ain't got no home, I'm just a ramblin' 'round,*
> *I'm just a wand'rin worker, I go from town to town.*
> *Police make it hard wherever I may go,*
> *And I ain't got no home in this world anymore.*

My brothers and my sisters are stranded on this road;
It's a hot, dusty road that a million feet have trod.
Rich man took my home and he drove me from my door
And I ain't got no home in this world anymore.

I was farmin' on the shares and always I was poor,
My crops I lay into the banker's store;
My wife took down and died upon my cabin floor
And I ain't got no home in this world anymore.

I mined in your mines and I gathered in your corn;
I been working, mister, since the day that I was born.
Now I worry all the time like I never did before
'Cause I ain't got no home in this world anymore.

The last verse emphasized Woody's view of the situation:

Now as I look around it's mighty plain to see
This wide and wicked world is a funny place to be.
The gambling man is rich and the working man is poor,
And I ain't got no home in this world anymore.

The camps were a rich source of inspiration for Woody. Conditions *were* awful, and it pained him to see so many people suffering. But there was a spirit in the camps that captivated him — a sense of unity, of brotherhood in the midst of chaos. The last thing he had expected to discover in the camps was beauty, so when it appeared he marveled over it. In one camp, it took the form of young voices singing.

"I heard these two girls from a-ways away, where I was leaning back up against an old watering trough," he recalled. "I could hear their words just as plain as day, floating all around in the trees and down across the low places. I hung my guitar on a stub of a limb, went down and stretched myself out on some dry grass, and listened to the girls for a long time....I just reared back and soaked in every note and every word of their singing. It was so clear and honest sounding, no Hollywood put-on....These songs [said] something about our hard traveling, something about our hard luck, our hard get-by, but the songs say we'll come through all of these in pretty good shape, and we'll be all right, we'll work, make ourself useful."

Woody Sez

 oody and Mary were growing more distant every day. While Mary struggled to raise two small children on dwindling funds, Woody waltzed in and out of their lives. When he was around, he was preoccupied with song writing, or rambling on and on about political events and unions and Communists. It made Mary's head spin. Sometimes she was actually relieved when he headed out the door.

In the fall of 1938, Culbert Olsen was elected governor of California. Because the Communists had helped win him the election, Olsen soon did them the favor of freeing labor activist Tom Mooney, who had served almost twenty years in prison for planting a bomb in a crowded San Francisco street. Mooney's trial and conviction, like Joe Hill's, had been based on weak, circumstantial evidence, and there was great rejoicing among the Communists when he was freed. Woody wrote a song for the occasion, called "Mr. Tom Mooney is Free," and he sang it for Ed Robbin, a Communist writer who had his own show on KFVD. Robbin immediately recruited Woody to perform it at an upcoming Communist Party meeting, and the audience went crazy.

Much of Woody's appeal among the Communists stemmed from his ability to write lyrics spontaneously, lyrics addressing political issues and events — even common, everyday situations. But his Dust Bowl origins were another big attraction, as many of the political organizers — most of them city born and bred — were infatuated with Woody's "hillbilly" roots. They often treated him more like a mascot than an equal, which didn't bother Woody one bit. He made the most of it, frequently feigning ignorance and country simplicity to bolster his popularity. Soon he was performing at a variety of Communist party functions and contributing a brief column to the *People's World,* one of the party's publications.

Around this time, Woody met Will Geer, an actor and activist who was touring West Coast migrant camps, and a friend of Geer's named Cisco Houston. The men had heard several of Woody's KFVD broadcasts and, enchanted, had gone to the station and introduced themselves. Cisco soon began hanging around, helping Woody open the letters that continued to flow into KFVD and singing along on some of the songs. Cisco was handsome and tall, with a graceful masculinity and a beautiful clear tenor singing voice. He was taken with Woody's lyrical abilities and unsophisticated style, and with his sense of humor, which complemented his own. The two became fast friends.

Shortly after their meeting, Geer persuaded Woody to join him as he continued to tour the camps and dramatize the benefits of unions. Though neither man was an official member of the Communist party, their hearts were with the workers and with the people who were risking their freedom—sometimes their lives—to improve the migrants' lot. They traveled from camp to camp, erecting flimsy stages upon which Geer—a veteran of Broadway— usually acted the role of the villain (often a heartless landowner) and Woody provided the musical entertainment.

For some time now, Woody had been maturing as a performer, gaining confidence, polishing the jokes and stories he told, and perfecting his timing. But the migrant audiences drew his best performances. He seemed utterly natural and completely relaxed before them, as though he were playing for a group of close acquaintances. And the truth was, he did consider the migrants friends, not followers, and hung around after the performances to get to know them a little better. "I made it my business to go into lots of the tents and shacks," he later wrote, "and hear them all sing, the little sisters, brothers, yodelers, ma and pa in the old [yellow] light of a coal oil lamp."

Geer also shone more brightly in these performances. The skits made both men feel less like artists working in isolation and more like citizens of the world, helping to shape—maybe even improve—the future. They weren't the only artists involved with the migrants, by any means. A number of folks had heard about the awful conditions of the camps, about the scarcity of jobs, and had come to witness the situation themselves. In the spring of

1939, a writer named John Steinbeck published a book that rocked the nation. It was called *The Grapes of Wrath.*

As a novel, the book was technically fiction. But Steinbeck had worked in the fields himself, living among the migrants, and his characters rang true. Their predicament echoed the plight of all the people trapped without money or livelihood in California. *The Grapes of Wrath* tells the story of the Joad family, "tractored out" of Oklahoma by the big land interests and forced west in search of a new life. The family travels to California, moving from one migrant camp to the next. When young Tom kills a vigilante who has murdered one of the family's closest friends, the authorities go after him, and the family is forced to separate in order to protect him.

The book created an instant furor. Associated Farmers pressured California booksellers and libraries to ban it and, in at least one county in the state, succeeded. But there was such an outcry throughout the rest of the country, as people began reading of the incredible poverty and brutality the migrants faced, that Congress convened a special committee to investigate labor practices and living conditions in California and the Pacific Northwest.

Woody was writing about the migrants, too — in letters home, in notebooks he carried with him, and in his songs. And he continued to write about them for several years. To him they were familiar people — not strangers to be puzzled over and not a "problem" that could eventually be made to disappear. "You've seen a million people like this already," he wrote, addressing his words to the average American. "Maybe you saw them down on the crowded side of your big city; the back side, that's jammed and packed, the hard section to drive through. Maybe you wondered where so many of them come from, how they eat, stay alive, what good they do, what makes them live like this? These people have had a house and a home just about like your own, settled down and had a job of work just about like you. Then something hit them and they lost all of that. They've been pushed out into the high lonesome highway, and they've gone down it.... Ain't much difference between you and them."

Meanwhile, war threatened the world. In Germany, under Adolf Hitler's leadership, the Nazi party was tightening its grip, expanding the military and enacting rigid controls over the lives of citizens. The Nazis were blatantly racist. They blamed their economic woes and other problems on the Jews and believed the Aryan race was superior to all others. As the decade drew to a close, the Nazis began striking out beyond Germany's borders, claiming Austria in 1938 and a large portion of Czechoslovakia later the same year. Americans watched these events closely, nervously. Barely twenty years had passed since World War I had ended. Were they in for another global confrontation?

Woody was more concerned with the problems immediately at hand: earning a living for his own family and helping to end the exploitation of the migrants. When the Soviet Union signed a nonaggression pact with Germany in August of 1939, Woody was shocked but not deterred from his goals. Under the terms of this pact, the Russians agreed to remain neutral even if Hitler launched assaults against other nations, and Hitler agreed to leave the Soviet Union alone.

But the pact stunned most Americans, including many Communists, who had long admired the stamina and perseverance of the Russian workers in establishing a new, proletarian government. Now, it seemed, the Russians had signed a pact with the devil himself. Thousands of members left the Communist party, which had only recently begun to enjoy some popular support.

To Woody, the events in Europe seemed too far away to concern him very much. "Now it looks like there are some wars breaking out around over the world," he wrote in a letter to his sister Mary Jo. "This is between the rich people. Us poor folks have nothing in the world to do with these wars, because, win, lose, or draw, we are poor to commence with, and will be poor to end with." He continued to perform at party functions and contribute his "Woody Sez" columns to the *People's World*. Though he was still not an official Communist, he believed the party offered the best hope for unskilled workers, who needed jobs and decent food regardless of what happened in Europe. Hitler might be the devil incarnate, but it seemed to Woody that the Russians had had little choice but to make their peace with him. If they hadn't, Hitler might have turned his aggression toward them—at a time when they were still quite vulnerable. Less than two weeks after the pact was signed, Germany invaded Poland. In response, Great Britain and France declared war against Germany, and World War II began.

—

Though he had been glad to support the Communists in their efforts to organize the migrants, KFVD owner Frank Burke had

Woody and Mary Jennings Guthrie with children, Los Angeles, 1940.

never been a Communist himself. And when Russian leader Joseph Stalin signed his pact with Hitler, Burke became completely disillusioned and disgusted. It galled him that Woody continued to affiliate with Communists, and it disturbed him even more that Woody was hyping their cause over KFVD airwaves.

Shortly after the pact was signed, the Soviet Union became aggressive itself, dividing up the Polish territories with Germany and, in November, invading the neighboring country of Finland. When Woody remained loyal to the Communists, his relationship with Burke collapsed completely, and his KFVD show ended.

Will Geer had headed back to New York to play the leading role in a New York theater production, so Woody was on his own again. Communist audiences — agitated by the events taking place in Europe — began to tire of his hillbilly banter and cornball humor. Woody's own responsibilities were heightening. Mary had recently given birth to their third child, a son, named Will Rogers Guthrie. Without Geer's influence, and lacking a regular radio outlet, Woody's popularity began to wane. It wasn't long before he packed up the family and headed back to Texas.

But Woody was even more unpopular in Pampa. In fact, he was practically an outcast. Family and friends were angry over his treatment of Mary and the kids, over the way he would deposit them at the homes of various relatives and then disappear. On top of that, Woody's Communist sympathies were widely known in Pampa, and the townsfolk avoided him as much as possible. Woody was bored and a little hurt. Scarcely a month passed before he grew restless again. Will Geer had suggested he give New York a try one day. In early 1940, Woody decided to do just that.

CHAPTER 15

The Big Time

We loaded in a taxi to haul us crost the town
And it registered a nickel everytime the wheel went 'round
He charged us 'leven dollars and eighty-seven cent
And down in Texas that's enough to pay six months of rent
——FROM WOODY'S "THE NEW YORK TRAINS"

ew York City was mind-boggling. Huge and sophisticated, ever-wakeful, a blend of natives and immigrants, it proved to be the perfect antidote to Pampa. Woody marveled over the crowds, the "street cars [that] run under the ground up here, ['cause] they ain't got room for any more on the streets," and all the money changing hands. He moved in temporarily with Will Geer and his wife Herta, then relocated to the apartment of singer Burl Ives, whom he had met in California. Finally he rented a shabby hotel room of his own.

He began to explore the different neighborhoods of the city, especially the poorer sections. He discovered the Bowery, lined with alcoholics, and the Lower East Side, with its crowded tenements and squalid streets. In Times Square he found gangsters, panhandlers and assorted derelicts. And with the merchant seamen who docked at Manhattan's West Side water terminals, among whom he felt most comfortable, he began to frequent the bars of Hell's Kitchen.

Though the United States hadn't entered the war in Europe, it was shipping arms to Great Britain. After a long decade of depression, the country's factories were beginning to produce again—

mostly weapons and war machines — and the result was more jobs. The radio stations played popular tunes and patriotic songs, neither of which appealed too much to Woody. As far as he was concerned, pop tunes were based on fantasy, not reality, and he had little use for them. And the patriotic songs bothered him because they focused on flags and armies instead of the people who actually kept the country going. Whenever he heard a jukebox playing "God Bless America," it really grated on his nerves. Why, it hardly mentioned people at all! One night he got so fed up he started a patriotic song of his own. He wanted it to be a tribute to the beautiful countryside and vast resources of the nation. But he also wanted to assert the people's rights to that countryside. He wrote:

> *This land is your land, this land is my land*
> *From California to Staten Island*
> *From the Redwood Forest, to the Gulf Stream waters*
> *God Blessed America for me.*

The song, which Woody called "God *Blessed* America," had several verses. And it would undergo a number of revisions by the time he was finished with it, though its defiant spirit never wavered. A few years later he changed the name of the anthem to "This Land Is Your Land." It would become his most famous song.

Even after Woody moved out of his apartment, Will Geer tried to look after him. Because he was prominent in theatrical circles as well as in left-wing politics, Geer managed to line up several engagements. In early March, Woody appeared at the Forrest Theater in a benefit for the West Coast migrant workers. Several other notable musicians were listed among the evening's performers, including Aunt Molly Jackson, Huddie Ledbetter (better known as "Leadbelly"), and Alan and Bess Lomax. A talented young banjo player named Pete Seeger was also in attendance that evening. Later he wrote about the "little, short fellow with a western hat and boots, in blue jeans and needing a shave, spinning out stories and singing songs that he had made up himself. His manner was laconic, offhand, as though he didn't much care if the audience was listening or not."

But the audience *was* listening. And so were the other musicians, particularly Alan Lomax who, at only twenty-three, was assistant

Alan Lomax (Courtesy National Archives, Department of War Information).

director of the Library of Congress' Archive of Folk Song. Lomax was struck by Woody's unadorned sincerity and simple mastery of the American ballad tradition. He wasted no time inviting Woody down to Washington, D.C., for a recording session at the Library of Congress, and Woody eagerly accepted.

The session began on March 21, with Lomax's introduction, partially muffled by Woody's steady guitar strum and mournful harmonica: "'Lost Train Blues'— played on the harmonica and the guitar by Woody Guthrie from Okemah, Oklahoma." Over the course of the next three days, Lomax and his wife, Elizabeth Littleton, interviewed Woody about Okemah and Pampa, dust storms, labor contractors, the migrant camps, and early influences. Woody punctuated his answers with his own songs, a few traditional tunes, and wry anecdotes — his sense of humor shining through from the very beginning.

"Had some pretty rich oil fields around there," Woody remarked early on, referring to Okemah.

"Did any of the oil come in your family?" Lomax wanted to know.

"Nope. No," Woody replied. "We got the grease."

Later Lomax inquired about the origin of the song "Chain Around My Leg."

"When did you make that one up, Woody?"

"This'n?"

"Yeah."

"Yesterday up in your office," Woody answered, with a little chuckle.

"What?" Lomax sounded surprised.

"Yesterday up in your office," his prolific guest repeated.

Lomax had many musical connections in New York, and soon began looking for opportunities to showcase Woody's talents. Because he was a regular contributor to the CBS radio show "Columbia School of the Air," he arranged a guest spot for Woody in early April, paying him the grand sum of $200 — a fortune, as far as Woody was concerned, especially for a single performance. Later the same month, Woody was offered $50 to sing "Do Re Mi" on another CBS show, "The Pursuit of Happiness."

Then, in May, Lomax worked a miracle — or so it seemed to Woody. Victor Records agreed to record a selection of Woody's Dust Bowl material for commercial distribution. *The Grapes of Wrath* had recently been made into a successful motion picture, and the company hoped to capitalize on its popularity. In addition to Woody's existing Dust Bowl songs, the Victor folks asked him to write a song about *The Grapes of Wrath*. Woody was happy to comply. The resulting ballad, which he called "Tom Joad" (after the movie's protagonist), was written in a single sitting that lasted most of one night. It was a long ballad — almost twenty verses — that recounted the Joads' whole story in simple, straightforward lyrics, including the family's arrival in California:

They stood on a mountain and they looked to the West
And it looked like the promised land;
That bright green valley with a river running through,
There was work for every single hand, they thought,
There was work for every single hand.

Things were going well for Woody. After recording *Dust Bowl Ballads* for Victor Records, he and Pete Seeger traveled to Pampa to visit Mary and the kids, stopping in Oklahoma City to sing for some oil workers and folks without jobs. Returning to New York, Woody got several gigs playing in nightclubs—sometimes with Cisco Houston, who had recently come to town. But Leadbelly's apartment was Woody's favorite place to be. He passed so much time there that he usually wound up spending the night. He had never met anyone like Leadbelly before. A proud man of African-American heritage and twenty-five years older than Woody, he had learned hundreds of work songs, spirituals and blues during his early years in Louisiana and Texas. Woody loved to watch his muscular hands work music out of his big twelve-string guitar, and to listen to his husky voice croon the blues. "He had a slow running, easy, deep quiet way about him," Woody wrote, "that made me see that his strength was like a little ball in his hands....The first few days that I stayed around Leadbelly's house I didn't even ask him how old he was....I didn't ask too many questions, because I didn't know where to start." But as the weeks passed, Woody learned a lot from Leadbelly, both musically and otherwise. Despite their obvious differences, the two had a lot in common, most importantly their love for the music of their forebears.

Meanwhile, radio offers continued to roll in. In August, Woody sang "So Long, It's Been Good to Know Yuh" (originally called "Dusty Old Dust") on Alan Lomax's new CBS show, "Back Where I Come From." Shortly afterward, the network asked him to sign on as a regular performer at a salary of $150 a week. Among the other offers was a chance to host a weekly show sponsored by the Model Tobacco Company, a program called "Pipe Smoking Time"—for $200 a week! The offers were coming so fast and the dollar amounts were getting so high, Woody could hardly take it all in. Of course, he'd performed on the radio back in Los Angeles, but this was different. New York was the big time, with national

Leadbelly entertaining youngsters in the mid-1940s (Courtesy LSU in Shreveport, Noel Memorial Library, Department of Archives and Special Collections).

audiences from all walks of life. And the money! It just couldn't be beat. Woody stood poised to rake in several hundred dollars a week, a fortune by 1940 standards.

At first he was ecstatic. After all, it was nice to be appreciated. But soon the pressures started to build. Though he was drawing all kinds of mainstream attention, his politics hadn't changed. In addition to his radio spots and other public appearances, he wrote a regular column for the *Daily Worker* and performed at various Communist party functions. In fact, since his arrival a few short months before, he'd become wildly popular among New York City radicals. His heart still lay with the workers and the union organizers. They were the folks who were doing the important work, he felt, and he wanted to contribute.

It wasn't long before word began trickling out that Woody hung around with Communists, and it made him a little nervous. It was only a matter of time before the big companies that sponsored his radio shows found out, and they were bound to be unhappy about it. Woody felt torn. On the one hand, his songs were getting national attention, reaching people he would never have the opportunity to meet otherwise. On the other hand, if his sponsors couldn't accept his politics, was it really worth it? Woody didn't know what to do. In October, the pressure grew so intense he lost his cool. He quit writing the columns for the *Daily Worker,* then felt so guilty he stormed out of his job on "Back Where I Come From." But Lomax intervened, calmed Woody down, and convinced him to return to the program.

"Pipe Smoking Time" began broadcasting in November, and Woody immediately sent for Mary and the kids. They rented a four-room apartment, complete with piano, and had money to burn. They hired sitters for the kids and went out on the town several nights a week. The rest of the time they entertained a steady stream of visitors at home. Woody was happy — at first. But then he began to sour on the scene.

For one thing, the Model Tobacco folks weren't taking any chances. They gave Woody a script each week and expected him to stick to it — no extemporaneous speaking. And they changed around "So Long, It's Been Good to Know Yuh" until it was just an advertisement for their product. Woody had no creative freedom at all, and that bugged him more and more each day. The longer he stayed with the show, the guiltier he felt. He'd started writing songs because he had something to say — not because he wanted to make money. Now his songs were being altered or ignored altogether, and the only thing he had to show for his pains was cash. For Woody, it wasn't nearly enough. "I never sung or made one ballad song to entertain you," he later wrote.

> I made all of my stuff to tell you and
> To educate you.
> I'm an educator
> Not any entertainer.

By the end of the year, he had reached his limit. Shortly after New Year's Day, 1941, he announced to Mary that they were leaving New York.

CHAPTER 16

Along the Green Valley

Woody couldn't get out of New York City fast enough. The noise, the crowds, the relentless pace of life — all were suffocating him. So he packed up the family and headed to El Paso, Texas, where Matt Jennings had recently settled. No sooner had they arrived when Woody took off again — this time for the Chisos Mountains with Mary's brother Fred. He wanted another chance to find his grandfather's silver mine — at least that's what he told the others. Mostly, he just needed some space to himself. It made him glad to see the mountains again, the way the light drizzled across the foothills. The desert itself was silent and ageless and majestic. Gradually, it worked its magic, and the raucous memory of New York began to fade.

Returning to El Paso, he picked up his family and continued west to California, stopping when they reached the sleepy, mostly empty community of Columbia, an old gold rush town. Alan Lomax had suggested he write an autobiography and, now that his days were free, he began working on it. But within a couple of weeks he grew restless again. Now the family headed to Los Angeles, where Woody planned to reclaim his post at KFVD.

Many things had changed since Woody had last lived in the state. For one thing, the migrant camps had vanished from the central valley. The war in Europe had created jobs in California, too — and plenty of them, mostly in defense plants. The growers had started hiring Mexican laborers again to pick their fruit. When the season ended, they sent the workers back to Mexico. And Frank Burke had no intention of re-hiring Woody.

The family was stranded, lacking a plan for the future, and unable to find a house to rent that accepted children. Mary was fed up, tired of bouncing from one city to the next, and said so. She wanted a home of her own, a place where the children could grow up peacefully, where they wouldn't have to pick up and move every few months. She and Woody began to quarrel again, their arguments growing fiercer by the day.

Finally, Woody called his old friend Ed Robbin, who helped them find a place to stay and made a few suggestions about making money, too. But Woody was beginning to regret his hasty departure from New York. It wasn't the city that he missed so much, though he sure could use the money now. No, what he missed were his friends: Leadbelly, Pete Seeger, Cisco Houston, Lomax. For the first time in his life, Woody had been connected to a circle of people who understood his music, who valued him. And here he was stuck on the opposite coast, his marriage falling apart around him. What was he going to do now?

Woody made it through the next few weeks by the skin of his teeth, scraping up a few dollars playing at fund-raisers and other events. Then he heard he was being considered for a role in a documentary film about a huge new dam on the Columbia River, near Portland, Oregon, so he and the family journeyed north. He was dead broke, having gone through all his New York money, and the movie seemed his last hope. By the time he arrived at Bonneville Power Administration headquarters, the future of the film project had already been cast in doubt. Instead of a movie role, Woody was offered a job writing songs about the Grand Coulee Dam, then under construction, which would bring electricity to rural areas of the state. The BPA hoped Woody's songs would help advertise the dam and rally people behind the project.

Woody was enthusiastic. There were thousands of migrant workers still stranded in the Pacific Northwest, folks who had fled the northern Great Plains during the Depression. Unlike their neighbors in California, who had found jobs in the burgeoning defense industry, many of these migrants still lacked employment and were forced to make their homes in abandoned farmhouses, weatherbeaten shacks, empty lumber camps, even makeshift shelters erected to store fruit. This new dam, financed by the government, would create jobs and help end the terrible poverty in which these people lived. As far as Woody was concerned, it was exactly the kind of project the government should be sponsoring, because it helped *people* instead of big business. Woody accepted the job immediately. He would be paid $260 a month, provided he produced a song—or part of a song—each day.

He spent his time traveling up and down the river, watching the water flow past, talking to the workers, daydreaming, scribbling in notebooks. He hadn't written many songs lately, with his life so hectic. But now the words began to pour forth in a steady stream, like the river he was writing about. As he had in the past, he borrowed most of his melodies from traditional tunes, then added his own lyrics. He wrote about the power of the river, about jobs, about the difficulties of life on the road, about the dam itself. And he didn't mind exaggerating if it made for a better song, as in "The Grand Coulee Dam":

Well, the world has seven wonders that the trav'lers always tell,
Some gardens and some towers, I guess you know them well,
But now the greatest wonder is in Uncle Sam's fair land,
It's the big Columbia River and the big Grand Coulee Dam.

Many of his songs had little or nothing to do with the dam. Most of them dealt with work, from mining to pressure-drilling to pouring steel. Some of his most poignant songs talked about the life he knew best: the life of the migrants, who had lost their farms and their livelihoods and traveled hundreds of miles on sheer hope. For "Pastures of Plenty," he borrowed the melody of a murder ballad called "Pretty Polly," modifying it a bit and adding lyrics that changed it from the mournful tale of a helpless victim to a powerful tribute to the migrants' hard work and devotion:

It's a mighty hard row that my poor hands have hoed;
My poor feet have traveled a hot dusty road,
Out of your dust bowl and westward we roll,
And your desert was hot and your mountain was cold.

I've worked in your orchards of peaches and prunes,
Slept on the ground in the light of the moon,
On the edge of your city you've seen us and then,
We come with the dust and we go with the wind.

California and Arizona, I make all your crops,
And it's north up to Oregon to gather your hops,
Dig the beets from your ground, cut the grapes from your vines,
To set on your tables your light sparkling wine.

Green pastures of plenty from dry desert ground,
From that Grand Coulee Dam where the water runs down,
Every state in this Union us migrants have been,
We work in your fight, and we'll fight till we win.

Well, it's always we ramble, that river and I,
All along your green valley I'll work till I die,
My land I'll defend with my life, if it be,
'Cause my pastures of plenty must always be free.

By the end of the month — one of the most productive months of his life — Woody had written twenty-six new songs.

Even after leaving New York City, Woody kept in touch with Pete Seeger, who liked to sing and play the banjo. And like Woody, who had already influenced him profoundly, Pete preferred songs that had some relevance to everyday life — not simple pop tunes. In early 1941, about the same time Woody fled New York City, Pete met Lee Hays, a preacher's son from Arkansas, a marvelous singer with a rich, booming, bass voice. He was also a talented lyricist, especially when it came to attaching his political messages to the melodies of traditional hymns. Pete and Lee joined up with a clever young writer named Millard Lampell and began calling themselves the Almanac Singers. Most of the songs they wrote and performed concerned the labor movement, or urged peace in the face of World War II — an increasingly unpopular stance at the time. While most Americans hoped England would defeat Germany, many folks on the political Left thought differently. Some were pacifists, opposed to any war. Others, particularly the Communists, thought England seemed more intent on turning Germany against the Soviet Union than on ending Hitler's murderous crusades. After all, just a few years earlier, when Hitler-backed Fascists had tried to overthrow Spain's legally elected government, neither England nor the United

States had voiced any objections—and now they were condemning fascism in any form! For many leftists, the facts just didn't add up.

Soon after forming their group, the Almanacs rented an apartment big enough for the whole assembly, which sometimes included Sis Cunningham, Pete Hawes, Bess Lomax (Alan's younger sister) and Arthur Stern. By pooling their income and expenses, it would be easier to survive. It would also be easier to rehearse and to write material if they all lived in one place. To earn the rent money, they began giving concerts once a week. Though their income remained meager, their popularity rose steadily. By summer, they decided, they'd be ready to take their songs directly to "the people," and they began planning a cross-country tour. When Germany invaded the Soviet Union on June 22, they abandoned their peace songs altogether and focused on labor material. They also began writing songs about beating the Fascists. Hitler had to be stopped at any cost. War seemed the only solution.

Woody corresponded frequently with Pete and the others. This new group they had formed—named after a farmer's most practical book—sounded too good to be true. When he heard the Almanacs were planning to travel cross-country, he decided to join them. As soon as his contract with BPA expired, he hitched a ride to New York City, leaving Mary and the kids behind in Portland.

The Almanacs began their tour in Philadelphia, where they played at an Independence Day rally before moving on to Pittsburgh. They sang for the National Maritime Union in Cleveland, for striking furriers in Chicago, and for members of the CIO in Milwaukee. In Minneapolis, they joined a picket line with workers on strike from International Harvester. At each stop on the tour, they were housed by local union members or other political organizers, who were more than happy to describe regional working conditions. Some nights they stayed up late writing new material, with each member of the group receiving equal credit and equal pay. By the time they reached San Francisco, the last stop on the tour, they were ebullient. For more than a month, they'd been in the thick of the country's labor movement. They'd not only sung about it, they'd experienced it firsthand—in some cases they'd even influenced it. Often they'd entered union halls full of tired, unruly workers, some of whom had even scoffed as the four Almanacs moved to the front of the room. But after a few

The Almanac Singers. From left: Woody, Millard Lampell, Bess Lomax, Pete Seeger, Arthur Stern and Sis Cunningham.

rousing choruses of a song like "Union Maid," the entire assembly was on its feet, cheering and singing along:

> *Oh, you can't scare me, I'm sticking to the union.*
> *I'm sticking to the union, I'm sticking to the union.*
> *Oh, you can't scare me, I'm sticking to the union.*
> *I'm sticking to the union till the day I die.*

Giddy with success, they extended the tour a few more weeks, spending most of the month of August in Los Angeles — without Lee Hays, who had returned east from San Francisco. In early September, growing tired, Millard Lampell dropped out, too.

Woody and Mary had been married eight years, with three blond children to show for it. Gwen, the oldest, was ready to start school. Now it was simply a question of where. Stranded in Portland, Mary grew impatient waiting for Woody to return. She was tired of counting on him, of being subject to his every whim, of having to raise three youngsters alone while her husband did as he pleased, obviously unconcerned. When the school year began in September, she packed her bags and set out for Los Angeles. Woody would have to change — by giving up his life on the road —

or she would leave him. It was as simple as that.

In Los Angeles she confronted him. Woody was startled by her vehemence but not about to change. He asked her to move back to New York with him but made it clear he would continue to travel — this union work was much too important to quit now. Mary wasn't interested. If she were going to be left alone again, she'd rather be alone in her own territory. She said her goodbyes and took the children to El Paso. Although it would be a couple of years before they were officially divorced, it was the end of their married life.

Even though Woody was sad about the split, it had seemed inevitable for some time. He loved Mary, but lately she hardly resembled the shy, sweet teenager he had married. He didn't understand the toll his irresponsibility had taken, but their troubles had other roots, too. To Woody, it seemed clear that they were headed down different roads in life. And he was angry that Mary "hated all of my new books and new friends and my newfound thoughts with a poison in her belly that killed everything I tried to learn and to work at faster even than I could tell her about them.

"The worst pity of our sad mismatch," he later wrote, "was that we had three small baby children, two girls and one little boy, to share the mental benefits of our mean despiteful and hateful kinds of arguments."

CHAPTER 17

Railroad Pete

few months after returning to New York, Woody got an important gig. A young choreographer named Sophie Maslow recruited him to play guitar for a piece she called *Folksay,* a series of movements set to poetry and folk music. Woody had agreed to play for Maslow a few months earlier, on another project, but it hadn't worked out. This time he would be accompanied by Earl Robinson, a prominent left-wing composer. In addition to backing up the dancers with songs, the two would tell several brief, folksy stories and jokes.

But there were problems. Maslow had choreographed her dancers' movements to *recorded* folk songs, and she expected Woody and Robinson to play the songs precisely as they had been recorded — or else the movements wouldn't fit. The task proved more difficult than anyone had imagined.

"It was here that I learned a funny thing," Woody wrote. "People that sing folk songs never sing them twice alike. If you're the same the weather's different and if the weather is the same and even if you're the same, you breathe different, and if you breathe the same you rest or pause different. The problem I had was to memorize these folk songs...exactly as they were on the records."

One of the women in the troupe was a tiny, delicate beauty named Marjorie Greenblatt Mazia. From the moment she and Woody met, there was a strange connection between them — an immediate bond. Marjorie noticed Woody having difficulty maintaining the proper rhythm and immediately devised a solution: She created flash cards with the song written out in beats, including the pauses.

"I figured a dancer with any sense at all could make a few quick changes and invent a few steps...in order to keep in step with my singing," Woody explained. But later "one girl told me the theater was like a factory. The people are like the wheels. If they don't all turn the same way at the same time, they'll tear each other up."

Woody tried Marjorie's system, and the situation improved, though not completely. "I would do all right for a while and then I'd miss a beat or put in a note too many and everybody would run over everybody else."

By opening night the problems had been ironed out, and the production went off smoothly. By then Woody's mind was occupied with other thoughts, all of them centering on Marjorie. He was hooked. He admired her physical strength and gentle grace, her intelligence and beauty. Before long he was spending as much time as possible with her — which wasn't much. Besides her part in *Folksay*, Marjorie had daily rehearsals with the Martha Graham Dance Company, which was gearing up for a national tour. She also had a husband in Wilmington, Delaware, though the marriage was an unhappy one. Because her work kept her in New York most of the time, she had rented a small room in the city. When spring came, Woody moved in with her — and stayed even after she left for the tour a few weeks later. He was working on his autobiography again. In fact, he had landed a publishing contract for the book, including a $500 advance — half of which went to Mary and the kids.

He was still performing with the Almanac Singers, too, though lately their bookings had been on the decrease. With the bombing of Pearl Harbor in December 1941, they had shifted all their creative energies to war songs. The United States had joined the other Allies fighting Japan, Germany and Italy, and the whole country was consumed with battle fever. The defense industry was escalating production, young men were being drafted into the military — or joining voluntarily — and unions were being pressured to stop all strike activity until the war was over.

For a while, the new repertoire paid off. The Almanacs were booked on network radio — even asked to audition for a stint at the Rainbow Room, one of New York's ritziest night spots. But Woody, for one, had learned his lesson. As soon as he glimpsed the other performers waiting to audition, eager to please and "smiling like

Woody with friends, New York City. At left is Brownie McGhee, with Woody beside him. Second from right is Sonny Terry.

they'd never missed a meal," he sickened. It reminded him of the Model Tobacco fiasco. When the Rainbow Room managers asked the Almanacs to don gunny sack costumes and exaggerate their hillbilly traits — to better entertain the rich customers — Woody and the others walked out of the audition without regrets.

In February of 1942, the Almanacs performed on "This is War," a national program broadcast over all four radio networks — the group's biggest exposure to date. Within a week of the broadcast, articles attacking the Almanacs' "Communist associations" began appearing in the New York newspapers. The articles questioned the Almanacs' patriotism and suggested the group be banned from the airwaves. Almost immediately the job offers stopped. Woody was outraged.

"If you play any part in getting money from the worker and giving it over to the owner, then you are an upright and true citizen," he wrote. "But if you play any part in getting money from the owner and giving it over to the worker, of course, the loud speakers and printed pages yell and scream that you are a wild man running loose with a pocket full of...bombs and a head full of communist ideas."

With the Almanacs in decline, Woody decided to start a new

musical group, so he turned to Leadbelly and two other folk musicians who had relocated to New York: blues guitarist Brownie McGhee and harmonica player Sonny Terry, a virtuoso who "blew and whipped, beat, fanned and petted" his instrument. They called themselves the Headline Singers.

In June, Marjorie discovered she was pregnant. Though she loved Woody, the father of her child, she didn't know what to do. After all, she was still married to someone else! And if she were to leave her husband, how would she support herself during the pregnancy? Woody's dependability seemed questionable. After considering her options, she made a tough decision: She would return to Wilmington for the duration of the pregnancy, to ensure her own and the baby's health, and then she would divorce her husband and return to New York. Both Woody and her husband agreed to the arrangement—an unusual one, particularly by 1942 standards. By summer's end, Marjorie had moved out of the rented room she shared with Woody, leaving him alone again.

As was his custom, he kept busy. He began a diary to his unborn child, whom he christened "Railroad Pete." Every day he recorded his thoughts and impressions, wrote about his loneliness for Marjorie, and attempted to educate his future child.

"Do you know what a hoper is?" he asked in one entry. "Well, that's what your mama is, a hoper. She has more hopes per square inch than almost anybody else."

As work progressed on his autobiography, he wrote about that. "Your mama and me are just holding our breath now and waiting to see what's going to happen to our book...which is now named 'Bound for Glory.'"

And war, too, worked its way into the diary. "Maybe I could talk to you about fascism," one entry began. "It is a big word and it hides in some pretty little places...."

One of the many drawings among Woody's "Railroad Pete" entries.

Sooner or later, just about every thought that crossed his mind made its way into the diary. When the topic of music came up, Woody's language became lush and poetic. "There's a feeling in music and it carries you back down the road you have traveled and makes you travel it again," he wrote in late summer 1942. "There never was a sound that was not music — the splash of an alligator, the rain dripping on dry leaves, the whistle of a train...the silent wail of wind and sky caressing the breasts of the desert." His words were full of feeling, urgency. Though he treasured all his children, he awaited this birth with a peculiar intensity. He wanted this child to understand him, to know everything he thought or remembered or hoped for the future. Sometimes he felt overcome by strange sensations that hinted at his own mortality and vulnerability. The diary was a way of cataloging the changes coming over him, and he poured his heart out to Railroad Pete.

In February of 1943, Cathy Ann Guthrie was born, and Railroad Pete faded out of existence. Woody and Marjorie rejoiced over their tiny daughter's health, over her "dancer's legs" (pointed out by Marjorie) and dark curls (which matched her father's). In their hearts and hopes, she embodied the best of them both and was living proof of their love for one another. After traveling to Wilmington to see his new daughter, Woody stood for a long time at the hospital nursery's observation window, trying to memorize as many details about her as he could. It would be several more weeks before Marjorie returned to New York.

The move was scheduled for mid-April. Marjorie planned to look for an apartment of her own, somewhere near her parents in Brooklyn, where she and Cathy would be safe and sheltered. She had decided to take her time about setting up a household with Woody. She prided herself on being strong and self-sufficient. And she sensed that Woody was beginning to feel pressured by the responsibility of providing for another child. More importantly, Woody seemed to have few money-making prospects of his own.

That changed fairly quickly. *Bound for Glory* had just been published, and the reviews were trickling in — most of them favorable. His publisher quickly offered him a contract for a second book, with another $500 advance, and in May he won a $1,700 fellowship from the Rosenwald Foundation. *The New Yorker* called him "a national possession, like Yellowstone or Yosemite," his photograph appeared in *Life* magazine, and network radio shows were booking him again. In a matter of weeks, he had become something of a celebrity. Then the U.S. Army caught up with him. Unless he joined the war effort voluntarily, the Army advised him, Woody would be drafted in June.

For several weeks now Cisco Houston had been trying to persuade him to join the Merchant Marines, a fleet of civilian ships that carried war supplies overseas. Though merchant seamen weren't part of the military, their service made them exempt from the draft. When the Army notice arrived in the mail, Woody finally capitulated. He and Cisco headed down to the National Maritime Union office and signed up for the *William B. Travis,* which would sail for Europe with a cargo of bombs in late June. Then Woody moved in with Marjorie. He wanted to spend as much time with her as possible before his departure. Though they rarely talked about their worries, each was secretly afraid they might never see the other again.

CHAPTER 18

A Nautical Life

side from missing Marjorie terribly, Woody quickly adapted to life at sea. After all the months spent writing and rewriting *Bound for Glory*—not to mention the difficulties surrounding Cathy's birth—he was ready for adventure. Instead of a highway, this time an ocean beckoned. It felt good to be around a group of men again, to be part of a larger movement, particularly the fight against Hitler. He even painted "This machine kills fascists" across the face of his guitar.

From the start, Woody occupied a special place aboard the *Travis*, for the other men soon realized he was "different." They felt protective of him, in part because of his small size, but also because he was really very childlike at heart. He had a limitless curiosity, a sense of playfulness and wonder, and an uncanny ability to dominate most situations with very little effort.

Woody spent most of his first day at sea building a "wind machine." Whittled from scraps of wood and fastened together with rubber bands and interlocking gears, the sculpture whirred and spun in the breeze. Woody mounted it on the railing near the stern and invited his shipmates to add to it. The next day the contraption sported numerous new propellers, two small figures who bobbed up and down as the gears turned, and a handmade hen with feathers that vibrated in the wind. The day after that, someone added a funnel that murmured when the wind blew through it and several humming pennywhistles. It became a shipboard ritual to gather near the wind machine each evening at dusk to review the latest additions and listen to Woody and Cisco play their guitars and sing. Music helped ease their longing for

home. And because most of the men had contributed to it, the wind machine added a soothing, personal presence.

But the voyage was a tense one. Though the *Travis* was part of a convoy of ships, only a few destroyers shielded it from the German submarines roaming the Atlantic. Several other ships in the convoy were hit by torpedoes. Woody watched them erupt into plumes of smoke and fire and slide beneath the indifferent sea.

In mid-July, the *Travis* reached Gibraltar, along the southern coast of Spain. Three weeks later it sailed to Palermo, Sicily, where it anchored for six weeks. The men passed the time playing cards and swimming in the harbor. Finally, in mid-September, the *Travis* received orders to proceed to the tiny country of Tunisia. Traveling without escorts, the ship was torpedoed as it neared the city of Tunis. Woody and most of his shipmates were sleeping when the missile hit, but the sheer force and sound of the blow woke them all. Soon the deck was swarming with confusion as the sailors, frightened they might be hit again, tried to figure out what to do. The rest of the night was quiet, and the ship remained afloat long enough to reach the port of Bizerte.

Shortly after Woody shipped out on the *Travis,* Marjorie rented a small apartment in Coney Island, Brooklyn, one long block from the beach. In November, when Woody returned, having completed his first voyage, he joined her there. Mermaid Avenue was a long row of two- and three-story houses beginning to show their age — peeling paint, missing shingles, weeds poking through the walks. The neighbors were mostly working-class folks — waiters, storekeepers, seamstresses, factory workers. Most, like Marjorie, were Jewish.

During the day, while Marjorie danced and gave lessons in the city, Woody looked after Cathy. If the weather was pleasant, he headed straight for the boardwalk. Along the waterfront, two amusement parks rose above the beach, and the area was crammed with hot dog stands, souvenir shops, penny arcades and snack counters. In the summertime, the beach was packed and boisterous. The rest of the year the rides and stands stood barricaded and quiet, and the boardwalk remained empty except for clusters of old men discussing the progress of the war. Woody hummed to himself as he walked along, pushing Cathy in her stroller, the wheels clicking rhythmically over the wooden planks. He was happy to be home again, most especially to be alive. He felt more deeply connected to his family, to his music, to the important things in life. "A torpedo knocks a lot of things out of you," he wrote, "and if you live through the shake up, it knocks a lot of new things into you. It puts a lot of your thoughts straighter in your mind, and sets your hopes and your plans up clearer and plainer."

But in January 1944, with the Army still threatening to draft him, Woody was forced to sign up for another voyage, this time to Algeria, in northern Africa, aboard the *William Floyd.* He was reluctant to leave his family again, and packed a typewriter and books and an assortment of musical instruments to help pass the time and take his mind off his loneliness. Though the voyage was quiet, Woody was horrified by the incredible poverty he witnessed in Algeria, which reminded him of the living conditions he had encountered in Sicily a few months before.

In Sicily, "every wall was either cracked, scarred, chipped or else completely smashed," he wrote. "Homes gaped open like blasted corpses, whole blocks of living quarters were ripped away, old

broken windows stared across the town, and appeared like shell-shocked eyes....the people like homeless ants. A thing of this kind has always been hard for me to describe."

Woody was so moved he gave most of his money away to children, knowing it would ease their suffering only a little — and all too briefly.

In early spring, having returned to New York, Woody heard talk that interested him deeply. A Jewish immigrant named Moses Asch ran his own studios on New York's West Side and was looking for folk musicians to record. Woody headed there at once, stepped inside Asch's offices and announced, "I'm Woody Guthrie."

Asch hadn't heard of him. Nevertheless, amused by Woody's brashness, he set up his equipment and invited the little man to play a few songs. Within a matter of minutes, Asch's attention was completely riveted. This fellow was the real thing! Over the next few weeks, with Woody's complete and enthusiastic cooperation, Asch recorded several hundred masters of his songs.

Then Woody was off to sea again, this time aboard the *Sea Porpoise*. On June 6, 1944, as the ship was crossing the Atlantic, news came over its radio that Allied troops had stormed the coast of Normandy, France, and were close to breaking the Nazis' ruthless grip on Europe. The men were ecstatic, and celebrations began immediately. Yet a sense of unspeakable danger hovered over the passengers and

Moses Asch (Courtesy Smithsonian Institution, Center for Folklife Programs).

95

crew. German submarines laced the deep waters of the Atlantic, hunting Allied vessels, and though the *Sea Porpoise* carried three thousand troops, there were enough lifeboats for only a few hundred. Woody and Cisco spent their nights far below deck, where the enlisted men traveled, organizing square dances and sing-alongs to distract the soldiers from their troubles.

Off the coast of Normandy, after the troops had been discharged from the ship, a mine ripped a huge hole in the side of the *Sea Porpoise*, the blast so terrific it sent Woody flying across his cabin. Again the vessel was strangely lucky, remaining above water long enough to be towed to Southampton, England, while the war raged about it. Though Woody and Cisco survived the ordeal, Woody's mind was made up: He was through with the Merchant Marines. No more of the nautical life for him! His resolve lasted about eight months, until the next Army induction notice arrived in the mail.

CHAPTER 19

Boot Camp

 ranklin D. Roosevelt was up for reelection in the fall of 1944. If he won the race, it would be his fourth term in office. No other U.S. president had served as long, and the campaign made lots of people nervous, particularly Roosevelt's opponents. Thomas Dewey, the Republican presidential candidate, called Roosevelt's supporters Communists and claimed they wanted, ultimately, to overthrow the government.

Many Communists *did* back Roosevelt, primarily because he had long supported the labor movement, but they weren't his only fans. Roosevelt had led the country through its darkest years — the Depression of the 1930s and now the horrors of World War II. He had restored a sense of hope, even if many of his programs had failed. With the war still going on, most Americans were reluctant to elect anyone else, "to change horses in midstream," as the Democrats put it. Woody, for one, was wholeheartedly behind the Roosevelt candidacy. In late September, he joined Will Geer, Cisco Houston and a number of other performers and musicians for the "Roosevelt Bandwagon," a tour designed to win the president his bid for reelection.

The Bandwagon turned out to be a disappointment, though it didn't keep Roosevelt from victory. In most of the towns the group visited, Woody and the others were mocked in the papers for their Communist ties and radical political ideas. Only the left-wing audiences were appreciative — but then, they would have voted for Roosevelt anyway. Woody was glad when the stint was over.

In December, he landed a weekly fifteen-minute spot at WNEW Radio. Though the show lasted only a few weeks before it was cancelled, Woody managed to imprint his personality right from the start. In his first broadcast, he outlined his attitudes toward music. "I hate a song that makes you think that you're not any good," he explained,

> I hate a song that makes you think that you are just born to lose. Bound to lose. No good to nobody. No good for nothing. Because you are either too old or too young or too fat or too slim or too ugly or too this or too that. Songs that run you down or songs that poke fun at you on account of your bad luck or your hard traveling.
>
> I am out to fight those kinds of songs to my very last breath of air and my last drop of blood.
>
> I am out to sing songs that will prove to you that this is your world and that if it has hit you pretty hard and knocked you for a dozen loops, no matter how hard it's run you down and rolled over you, no matter what color, what size you are, how you are built, I am out to sing the songs that make you take pride in yourself and in your work. And the songs I sing are made up for the most part by all sorts of folks just about like you.

It would become one of his most enduring speeches.

In March, at about the same time Moses Asch released an album of Guthrie songs (Woody's first since *Dust Bowl Ballads* several years earlier), Woody received another Army induction order. Failing to win a spot as one of the Army's "entertainment specialists," he reluctantly headed to the National Maritime Union offices to sign up for another stint with the Merchant Marines. To his amazement, his services were turned down. When he asked why, he was informed that his name was listed among members of the Communist party. Woody tried to explain that he wasn't a member of the party, though he readily admitted he had performed for many Communist functions, but the NMU wasn't interested. Woody returned home feeling stunned and a little angry. What made Communists unfit for service, anyway?

In early May, Woody was finally inducted into the Army and sent to boot camp at Fort Dix, New Jersey, the same day Hitler surrendered to the Allies. ("He must have seen me coming in," Woody wrote.) But Woody wasn't at all happy. For one thing, his uniform was several sizes too big. For another, he was at least ten years older than most of the other recruits — with four children to support on top of that. After Fort Dix, he was sent to Sheppard Field, in Texas, where he visited briefly with Mary and the kids, and then to Alton, Illinois, for teletype school. It was there, in August 1945, that he heard the news that World War II had ended with the Japanese surrender. Expecting to be discharged any day, Woody passed the time writing letters to Marjorie and his friends, including regular requests for money he directed to Asch.

"One reason why I have to write to you for money," he explained in one note, "is that I sit around and write letters to people that ask how to get ahold of folk records....This causes the chow bell to ring and also causes me not to make it and then causes me to have to eat my coffee in a canteen here for twenty cents. This happens three times a day which is sixty cents. This is eighteen dollars a month. I will only charge you fifteen dollars a month because Marjorie sends me three dollars...."

CHAPTER 20

Songs to Grow On

The little apartment in Coney Island was brimming with activity and crammed with belongings: musical instruments, mounds of paper, books, records, drawings, cartoons and homespun sculptures. Neighborhood kids dropped by all day, and Cisco Houston and other friends visited most evenings. Finally free from the Army after six long months, and newly married to Marjorie, Woody kept busy, trying to make up for lost time. Cathy was almost three now — a bright, happy child with her father's curly hair and bounding energy. Woody faithfully recorded her daily doings and sayings. "Took Cathy to school a piggy back this morning," he wrote. "She talked to everybody in the store and along the walk. She knows every window and all that is in it. She said one fellow had funny eyes."

From the time she was a baby, Woody had called his daughter, affectionately, "Stackabones"— or a variation of the name, such as "Stackaroony" or just plain "Stacky." While Marjorie taught dancing in the city, Woody often stayed home with Stacky. Every morning he perused the daily papers and wrote songs about the events described there, while Cathy drew pictures or made collages with colored bits of paper and string, or sea shells gathered from the beach. Other times they played records together — frequently recordings of Woody himself— and Cathy would dance and sing and ask, "How did they get you inside the music box, daddy?" Or Woody would strum his guitar and make up silly songs:

> *Why can't a dish break a hammer?*
> *Why, oh why, oh why?*

Because a hammer's a hard head.
Goodbye, goodbye, goodbye.

Why can't a bird eat an elephant?
Who, oh why, oh why?
Because an elephant's got a pretty hard skin.
Goodbye, goodbye, goodbye.

"Cathy plays a record."

He had always been too wrapped up in his own life to pay much attention to his children. But now that he was older, having survived the war and grown weary of distances, he marveled over the growth of this daughter. She was so open to the world, so endlessly creative, so curious about everything.

"Will the sun shine come and go with me to school every day or will the mean old clouds try to stop it?" she wanted to know. Woody would answer as best he could, sometimes reversing the situation and posing questions to Cathy, just to see what she would say. Though he was constantly writing letters, diaries and songs, the ditties he composed for Cathy gave him the most pleasure, primarily because they arose from his daily life with her — and because they entertained her so much:

Take me riding in the car, car,
Take me riding in the car, car,
Take you riding in the car, car,
I'll take you riding in my car.

At night, when Marjorie returned from dancing, Woody would rub her tired legs and feet and fill her in on the incidents of the day. He was giddy with love for this new family and full of admiration for his wife's accomplishments.

"Marjorie is small in size," he wrote. "Her hair is thick, shiny, curly and sparkles when she shampoos the big city soot out of it. Since the day she was born twenty-nine years ago she has kept

Marjorie Mazia Guthrie.

on dancing, except for a few weeks here and there of busted ankles, blistered feet, bones and muscles out-of-joint, and ligaments and gristles pulled out of socket. Even when her body was too bruised and broken, her face, her eyes, her mind has gone on dancing."

Coney Island fascinated him, too, particularly the mix of humanity that spilled over the beach once the weather got warm. Young and old, male and female, immigrant and native-born — all visited Coney Island, known as "the world's largest playground," in the summer season. Their laughter drifted above the boardwalk and mingled with the screams of roller-coaster riders. Swimmers raced through the cold surf, shrieking as the waves lapped against their bodies. Organ music pumped from the carousels. And vendors displayed every conceivable food, from watermelons to *knishes*. The rides had names like "Dragon's Gorge" and "Loop-o-Plane," and the sideshows advertised two-headed babies and snake-haired women. At night hundreds of thousands of lights twinkled and revolved above the waterfront, and happy voices populated the boardwalk. Along Mermaid Avenue where Woody lived, the older folks would sit in front of their houses and talk, calling out in sweet voices to their neighbors returning from work. At times like these, Coney Island did seem like the center of the universe. With all the movement and energy swirling about him and free from the rigid constraints of military life, Woody felt rejuvenated — and almost completely happy.

Of course there were problems, too, as in any life. Over the years Woody had continued to drink, sometimes quite heavily, and Coney Island didn't change that. Although Cathy and Marjorie were a kind of lifeline for Woody — making him feel more rooted than ever before — his old habits were hard to shake. Some days, knowing Marjorie was relying on him to watch Cathy, he would simply vanish, and Marjorie would have to scramble to make other arrangements. He hadn't gotten any better about money, either—not that he ever had very much. But when he did earn a few dollars, he was just as apt to give it away as to bring it home to his family. At times, frustrated over his slow progress on a second book, he became moody and quarrelsome. On such days, Marjorie actually preferred his absences to the high level of anxiety that permeated the apartment when he was around.

A few days after his Army discharge, Woody learned that Pete Seeger was back in New York, having served a stint in the military himself. Woody rushed to Greenwich Village, where Pete was staying with the family of his new wife, Toshi. "Pete walked down some steep stairs before Toshi could tell me where he was," Woody recalled. "Pete saw my guitar, unslung his banjo, and before we could shake hands or pass many blessings, we had played Sally Goodin, Doggy Spit a Rye Straw, Going Down This Road Feeling Bad, Worried Man Blues, and Fifteen Miles from Birmingham."

Then Pete told Woody about a new group he was forming, to be made up of people "who loved to sing folk songs and union songs," a group that would combat the syrupy jingles that passed for music in most parts of the country. The group was called People's Songs, and it hoped to stimulate greater interest in folk music by providing material to labor unions. Now that the war was finally over, dozens of strikes were breaking out across the nation. For more than four years the workers—not wanting to derail the war effort—had gone without pay increases, while factory owners' profits had skyrocketed. Now

With Pete Seeger (Courtesy Pete and Toshi Seeger).

From left: Lee Hays, Burl Ives, Cisco Houston and Woody.

the workers were clamoring for their fair share, and People's Songs intended to help them win it. Once the labor force was infused with folk music, the songs would flow on out to the masses, and a folk music revival would result — at least that's the way Pete and Woody and the other members of People's Songs saw it. Invitations for the group's first meeting went out to old friends and supporters, including Lee Hays, Oscar Brand, Mike Gold, Burl Ives, Millard Lampell, Alan Lomax, Earl Robinson and many others.

But after the first flurry of strikes, the unions quieted down and seemed to have little interest in the offerings of People's Songs. The environment had changed. Now that the unions were firmly established and no longer had to worry about being eradicated, their priorities shifted from educating and organizing the masses to collecting dues, electing officers, and developing internal policies and procedures. Some unions became quite hostile toward Communists and other left-wingers, even though the Communists had been a driving force behind the unions' creation.

But it wasn't only unions that had changed. The political climate of the whole country was different now. People were tired of struggle and agitation, having endured a long depression and almost five years of war. They wanted a little peace and quiet. They wanted the left-wingers to shut up, to quit clamoring for change. They wanted to settle down and raise families and bask in their hard-won security.

Even the world had changed. Though the Soviet Union had been a U.S. ally during World War II, it soon began forcing "Communist" governments (actually little more than dictatorships) upon a number of Eastern European countries and limiting contact with the western world. Western nations opposed its actions and began cutting ties in retaliation. Relations between East and West chilled considerably, launching a period called the Cold War.

But in the Guthrie household, the songs were genuine and an independent spirit thrived, infecting the country's newest generation. "Cathy dances only to a song when it is a Peoples Song," Woody bragged. And "she tells me that this holds good for every kid in her nursery school."

For three years now, ever since the publication of *Bound for Glory*, Woody had been struggling to complete his second book. He had already changed the subject matter and the title several times. At the moment it was called *Ship Story*, but his heart just wasn't in it. His focus was scattered in several different directions: remembering the war, trying to understand the new world, writing letters to newspapers and friends, taking care of Cathy, making up new songs, planning for the birth of another child in a few months. He was also recording his children's songs in Moses Asch's studio, which were eventually released in two albums: *Songs to Grow On* and *Work Songs to Grow On*. The simple refrains he had composed for Cathy were guileless and original — his best creations in several years — and he knew it. Marjorie was pleased, too, often accompanying him to the studio to help direct his performances, and Woody was grateful for her help. "I liked having Marjorie there," he wrote. "She tells me to sing it slow and plain, to vision Stacky Bones in my mind."

Cathy loved the albums, of course, as she had loved the songs from the moment of their creation. It heartened Woody to see their effect on his little daughter, who danced and sang and pounded on homemade drums. He envisioned the same joyous reaction in households across the country — for adults as well as kids. The songs had an important lesson to teach, he felt — a lesson Woody had learned long before. "Let your kids teach you how to act these songs out," he wrote in the album notes. "These and a thousand other songs....Watch the kids. Do like they do. Act like they act....I don't want the kids to be grown up, I want to see the grownups be kids." Woody didn't know it, but the harsh realities of the adult world would confront him all too soon.

CHAPTER 21

Walking the Lonesome Valley

t happened in 1947, on a cold Sunday in February, just a few days after Cathy's fourth birthday. Woody had gone to New Jersey to perform for a group of electrical workers. When he returned home, he smelled smoke and found a note instructing him to go to Coney Island Hospital. Immediately the old fear boiled up inside him. He rushed to the hospital in a panic.

At the emergency room, Marjorie broke the news: Cathy had been severely burned in a freak accident. She had been sitting on the family sofa listening to the radio when an electrical fire ignited, engulfing her. She was still alive, but deteriorating rapidly. Woody helped soothe her while the doctors worked to save her, but she died early the next morning.

Woody and Marjorie were stunned. It had happened so fast — in less than five minutes — and so inexplicably. Why should that radio burn up at that moment, with Cathy sitting beside it? Hardly anything else in the room was touched, just the sofa and the end table and a little section of wall. Marjorie felt responsible. She had left Cathy alone for those few minutes while she dashed across the street to buy some oranges. An upstairs neighbor had rescued the child, wrapping her in a blanket to smother the flames.

The loss struck Woody to the core, knifing through all the years that had transpired since Clara's fire and his mother's nervous collapse. It seemed to him that everyone he loved was doomed. Sometimes it even seemed that his loving them condemned them, and the pain and regret were overwhelming. That innocent little child, the source of so much joy and creativity, gone! Her absence gnawed at him even in his sleep. And the quiet house haunted him, until he could stand it no longer. In April he packed up a few belongings and headed west. He had to escape for a while.

A few weeks earlier, the Bonneville Power Administration had invited him to perform his Columbia River material at an April convention in Spokane, Washington. Now Woody decided to detour through Texas on his way to the convention, to visit old friends and relatives. But good as it was to see Uncle Jeff and Allene and his brother Roy, Woody began feeling depressed almost as soon as he arrived in Pampa. From his point of view, the town hadn't changed much. Racism still seemed widespread. Communists and progressives were reviled more than ever. Apart from their hatred of left-wingers, few people in town gave political and social issues much thought. Instead they focused on making a living, saving money. Woody felt like an outsider, as he had so long ago, and soon bid his kinfolks goodbye.

Spokane was different, full of life, its inhabitants open and curious about the future. While there, Woody made arrangements to perform for a number of left-wing groups along the West Coast, and shortly headed to Los Angeles. It felt good to be on the road again, among throngs of people, playing the union songs and talking to workers. But at the end of every day, his grief over Cathy loomed larger than ever, leaving him feeling unsteady and afraid. He wrote frequent letters to Marjorie, who had remained in New York and was growing more and more despondent. With this trip, Woody had hoped to revive the sense of adventure that had served him for so long. But the past was irretrievable, he now realized. There was only the present — and the future — waiting to be shaped. In mid-May, unable to hold his grief at bay any longer, he canceled his remaining bookings and headed home to Marjorie.

CHAPTER 22

"Go Back to Russia!"

he entire nation was down on Communists. With the war over, and a new period of prosperity ahead, Americans wanted to be rid of them. Communists were always talking about changing things and dividing up the nation's wealth—which had been a more popular idea when money was hard to come by. But now that most of the country was employed, with millions of workers protected by labor unions, the concept was rapidly losing its lustre.

In the spring of 1947, President Harry Truman issued Executive Order 9835, giving the government special authority to track down "disloyal" Americans and punish them accordingly. The Department of Justice began compiling lists of organizations deemed subversive or Communist in nature. People who associated with any of these organizations were prime suspects. Over the next five years, more than six million Americans were investigated as being possible Communist spies—though the actual membership of the American Communist party was only 100,000. The most famous Americans prosecuted at this time were Ethel and Julius Rosenberg, accused of espionage and later executed despite a trial marked by questionable legal practices and witnesses of dubious character.

Though he was still reeling from Cathy's death, Woody was aware of the nation's increasing intolerance, and deeply troubled by it. For several years now, he had been heckled for his Communist ties—and he was tired of it. "If your work gets to be labelled as communist or even as communistic or even as radically leaning in the general direction of bolshevism," he wrote, "then, of course, you are black balled, black listed, chalked up as a revolutionary bomb thrower." But he was smart enough to realize that the country would probably change its sentiments after enough years passed. It "ain't all good or all bad," he wrote. "Things happen fast, and change around...wars break out and folks are first on one side, then on another, because they believe in something, because they hate something, and because they get together with other people that think like they do."

Nothing made him angrier than seeing people lumped into categories because of their political beliefs, or because of their race or station in life — though when he was angry, he often blasted "rich folks" in the same unreasonable manner he abhorred in others. In his view, every person was unique and worthy of respect. He had particular empathy for people too poor to defend themselves and for people long excluded from the political process, such as African Americans and other minorities. He continued to read the papers regularly, to keep up with current events, and to write about the things he learned. When he heard that a plane had crashed while carrying Mexican migrant workers back to their homeland, killing all on board, he felt saddened. He was also shocked by the way the story played in the news — just a brief mention of the loss of a few nameless deportees. How dare their deaths be glossed over because they were poor! In a fit of outrage, he began writing about the accident, composing several verses that described the hardships of the migrant life, the plane crash, and the indignity of an anonymous death:

> *The crops are all in and the peaches are rotting,*
> *The oranges piled in their creosote dumps;*
> *You're flying 'em back to the Mexican border,*
> *To pay all their money to wade back again....*

> *The sky plane caught fire over Los Gatos canyon,*
> *A fireball of lightning, and shook all our hills,*
> *Who are all these friends, all scattered like dry leaves?*
> *The radio says they are just deportees....*

> *Is this the best way we can grow our big orchards?*
> *Is this the best way we can grow our good fruit?*
> *To fall like dry leaves to rot on my topsoil*
> *And be called by no name except deportees?*

Most haunting was the chorus, direct and full of feeling — a simple farewell:

Goodbye to my Juan, goodbye Rosalita,
Adios mis amigos, Jesus y Maria;
You won't have your names when you ride the big airplane,
All they will call you will be deportees.

Later, with a melody added, the song became known as "Deportee" — Woody's last great lyrical creation.

In July of 1947, Marjorie gave birth to a son, whom they named Arlo Davy. Woody's oldest daughter, Gwen, came up from Texas to visit, and the little apartment on Mermaid Avenue began to brighten again. A steady stream of neighborhood kids dropped by. From time to time, strangers appeared at the door — young men who had heard tales of Woody and wanted to meet him. If he was home, Woody usually invited them in and shared his music with them, often patiently showing them chords or picking styles. He was still working on his second book, but with renewed vigor. Now called *Study Butte*, it described his family's search for Jerry P. Guthrie's silver mine. He continued to perform for left-wing organizations, too, but most of his energy went into the book and his family. In 1948, another son, Joady Ben, was born. And a daughter, Nora Lee, arrived a year later.

People's Songs was still active, though bookings were getting fewer and farther between. In 1948, when Henry Wallace decided to run for president as a third-party candidate, Pete Seeger and several other members of the group threw their unqualified support behind him, performing at the Progressive party convention in July, at various rallies later that summer, and touring the South with Wallace in early fall. Both the candidacy and People's Songs' support of it were disasters. Wallace was criticized because many of his followers were Communists, former Communists, or left-wingers, and for several reforms he had initiated as Secretary of Agriculture under Franklin D. Roosevelt — reforms unpopular with big business. During Wallace's campaign swing through the southern states, some crowds were so hostile they threw eggs and tomatoes at him. When Election Day arrived, Wallace lost to

From left: Nora Lee, Joady Ben, Woody and Arlo Davy Guthrie, Coney Island, early 1950s.

Harry Truman by a huge margin, and People's Songs disbanded shortly thereafter.

Anti-Communist sentiment continued to mushroom. The CIO ejected all Communists from its membership, the entertainment industry was compiling lists of suspected party members, and many companies began requiring employees to sign loyalty oaths or face disciplinary action. The nation was obsessed. What had begun as a vague mistrust of left-wing radicals had become a fierce hatred, frightening in its proportions. In August of 1949, in Peekskill, New York, a mob attacked a group of people preparing for an upcoming concert by the great African-American baritone Paul Robeson, an admitted Communist who had spoken out on numerous political issues, often criticizing the United States for its discrimination against blacks. The attackers burned song books and pamphlets and planted a flaming cross in the ground. Robeson, refusing to be intimidated, set a new date for the concert. Woody, Lee Hays and many others made plans to attend.

Pete Seeger would be among the performers.

On the day of the concert, about one thousand union members traveled to Peekskill from New York City and surrounded the concert grounds to protect the performers. Yet even their presence was not enough to deter the angry mobs who had begun to mass, Pete recalled. As he approached the grounds with his family, including two very young children, he spotted an angry throng outside the entrance chanting, "Go back to Russia! Kikes! Nigger lovers!" But the crowd was roped off and there was a policeman stationed nearby, so he didn't worry too much. He proceeded to the stage, and the concert went on as planned.

Afterward, it took forever for the line of cars holding concertgoers, performers and union members to make its way out of the concert grounds. As Pete neared the exit, he found out why. Though there were three roads leading out of the area, two had been blocked off, and police officers were directing all cars down Division Street, the remaining road. As he inched along in the caravan of cars, Pete noticed some glass shards along the road.

"Oh-oh," he said to his family. "Be prepared to duck. Somebody may throw a stone."

The line of cars rounded the corner, and the figure of a young man became visible. He was standing next to a pile of stones "about waist-high," Pete recalled, with each stone "about as big as a baseball. And every car that came by got a stone — wham! — with all his force. And around the next corner was another pile of stones and another young man — altogether about ten or twenty piles of stones." Pete ordered his family to stay down. The windows of the car were already shattered.

Not far from one pile of stones, Pete spotted a policeman. The officer was calmly directing traffic, as though he hadn't noticed all the stones flying through the air and all the cars with busted windshields. Pete pulled up to the officer and stopped his car. He tried to roll down the window, but the splintered glass made that impossible. He did manage to roll it down far enough to address the lawman.

"Officer, aren't you going to do something?" he asked, finding it incredible that he had to ask. But the policeman ignored his question.

"Move on! Move on!" he directed, indifference lacing his voice.

Meanwhile, after the concert, Woody caught a ride back to

New York with Lee Hays and a friend. As they steered their car through the same gauntlet of angry men, with rocks and bottles smashing into their windows, Woody watched in horrified silence. These people were not so different from him. They had families to support, a future for which to prepare. Yet they were overcome with hatred for Robeson and Pete and all the people who had come to hear them sing. And the policemen stood watching the violence, doing nothing to halt it. What was the country coming to? Woody wondered. How could people hate complete strangers with such ferocity? After many long moments, he finally spoke, directing his words to no one in particular.

"I've seen a lot," he said, "but this is the worst."

Hard, Ain't It Hard

oody was acting strange, even for Woody. Though his behavior had never been predictable — aside from the fact that it was *always* unpredictable — it grew even more erratic in the weeks and months following the Peekskill "riots," as the attack came to be known. Close friends and family were beginning to remark about the change. After his latest manuscript was turned down by a publisher in the fall of 1949, Woody's concentration began to erode. He jumped from one activity to the next with little apparent interest in any of them. He disappeared more often and stayed gone longer, and when he returned his temper was short and his drinking heavy.

He yelled at Marjorie and the kids, from whom he had grown increasingly distant in the aftermath of Cathy's death. But the changes in his behavior ran even deeper than that. His sentences grew long and confusing and often impossible to follow. Sometimes his speech was slightly slurred, and when he walked his sense of balance appeared skewed. He continued to write songs, but none of his creations rivaled the originality and depth of his earlier works. He seemed to know it and was troubled by it. He grew increasingly despondent when he learned that Leadbelly, one of his dearest friends for almost ten years now, was seriously ill, suffering from Lou Gehrig's disease. In December of 1949, Leadbelly died.

Marjorie and the others attributed Woody's strange behavior to years of heavy drinking exacerbated by grief. Now he appeared intoxicated even when he was sober, but few folks felt much sympathy for him. He had had numerous warnings and opportunities for change over the years, all of which he had ignored. Though they still admired his talent, his friends began to avoid him as much as possible. It was easier than explaining the problems his strange behavior posed.

Pete Seeger saw Woody from time to time and was troubled by his deterioration. Because nobody had ever been able to control Woody's behavior, Pete didn't expect to have any luck at it, either, so he focused on other things. Even before the demise of People's Songs, Pete had been singing fairly regularly with a small group of friends. One of these was Lee Hays, whose strong bass voice and wide-ranging knowledge of folk music were impressive enough. But when he joined Pete, a young woman named Ronnie Gilbert (who sang contralto), and a versatile vocalist named Fred Hellerman, the result was remarkable. Their layered voices, punctuated by Pete's banjo and Hellerman's guitar, lent new drama and excitement to traditional folk songs. They decided to call themselves the Weavers.

A couple of months after the Peekskill riots, desperate for money and hoping to earn it with their musical abilities, the Weavers got a gig at the Village Vanguard, a New York nightclub where—to their complete surprise—they quickly became a hit. Within a matter of weeks they had a recording contract and a steady audience. One of their first singles, featuring Leadbelly's "Goodnight Irene," hit the top of the charts and stayed there for weeks, generating sales of more than two million copies. Although the various Weavers were thrilled at the record's success, they couldn't help remarking on the cruel twist of fate: Leadbelly had struggled all his life without ever achieving commercial success or economic stability. Now, less than a year after his death, "Goodnight Irene" was the most popular song in America.

The Weavers moved quickly to capitalize on their popularity, viewing it as an opportunity to bring folk songs to mainstream America. Though a number of their contemporaries accused them of watering down traditional songs to please the masses, Woody was happy to revise his own "So Long, It's Been Good To Know Yuh" for them, to make it appeal to a broad American audience. For his efforts, he received an advance of $10,000, which he and Marjorie needed desperately. They had recently moved to a larger apartment and were saddled with many old debts. The cash enabled them to catch up, buy a car, and finance Marjorie's own dance school, which she proudly opened in the fall of 1951.

Despite renewed success, Woody continued to deteriorate, suffering flashes of violence followed by periods of disorientation and remorse. After he charged at her with a knife one day, Marjorie became terrified he would hurt the children and began refusing to let him into the apartment. Woody would beg her forgiveness and promise to change, but sooner or later he would erupt again. Finally she asked him to leave for good.

He began traveling across the country again, taking a bus if he had the fare, hitchhiking or sneaking aboard trains if he didn't. He had never cared much about his appearance, but now he neglected it completely, sometimes going for days — even weeks — without shaving or taking a bath. In the spring of 1952, he traveled to Okemah to see a boyhood chum and spent several days walking through the town, visiting his hideout and other places from his youth, feeling suddenly old and inadequate. He was frightened by the changes taking place: his inability to think very clearly, the onrushes of aggression he felt, and the lack of control he had over his movements and gestures. Even his handwriting was deteriorating. Always very trim, it now grew huge and unwieldy, bulging over the edges of the paper.

Returning to New York, Woody spent most of his time trying to win his way back into Marjorie's good graces. He rented a small room in Manhattan, where he churned out letter after letter, begging her forgiveness and urging reconciliation. When he discovered she was dating someone else, he became violent again, sneaking into her apartment and attacking her when she returned. This time Marjorie called the police, who stayed until Woody calmed down. The next day, she accompanied him to Kings County Hospital, where he was admitted to a detox program for alcoholics.

Over the next several weeks, Woody checked in and out of hospitals. Even he assumed his problems stemmed from alcoholism, although one institution diagnosed him as schizophrenic. Between hospital stays he reverted immediately to his old habits — writing and telephoning Marjorie, paying unannounced visits to her apartment and, on at least one occasion, becoming violent again. Some nights he would ramble around the city, falling asleep in doorways or outside the apartments of old friends.

Deeply concerned for his safety — as well as the safety of her kids — Marjorie convinced him to check into Brooklyn State Hospital, where a new treatment called insulin shock therapy might improve his condition. Woody was given a battery of tests, and his behavior was carefully observed and documented. In early September 1952, the awful diagnosis came down: Huntington's chorea, a hereditary condition marked by personality changes, depression, impaired judgment, an intoxicated appearance, and a gradual decline in physical and mental functioning. Woody had inherited his mother's mysterious disease, for which there was no known cure.

CHAPTER 24

Green Pastures

When he was finally released from Brooklyn State Hospital, Woody headed to California. Marjorie had told him, in no uncertain terms, that their marriage was over. Though she still loved him deeply, she was worried about the children's safety and saw no other alternative. Horrified by his illness and overwhelmed by the darkness that now permeated his life, Woody sought escape. California had provided refuge in the past. Maybe it would again.

There were friends in California: Will Geer was there, and Pete Seeger and Lee Hays, as well as Cisco Houston. Woody stayed with Geer for a while, then bought several acres of land in Topanga Canyon. The nation was still censoring leftists, locking them out of most fields of employment, heeding the paranoid warnings of Senator Joseph McCarthy, who had declared all-out war against Communist "brutalitarianism." The Weavers had fallen victim to McCarthyism. And numerous other blacklisted artists had settled in the Topanga Canyon area, aiming to wait out the witch hunt. Most had heard of Woody Guthrie, the elusive folk singer and down-home philosopher who was already being compared by some to Will Rogers and Walt Whitman — much to his displeasure. "I ain't neither one," he argued. "Let those two rest in their silent sleeps and call me just by my own name."

Nevertheless, he aroused a good deal of attention and awe wherever he went. Within a matter of months, after getting a quick divorce from Marjorie, he had married a young woman named Anneke Van Kirk Marshall. Because Anneke hadn't known Woody before his illness set in, his tics and lurches weren't so apparent to her. In fact, for the first few months after Woody settled in California, the symptoms of Huntington's seemed to subside. But in the summer of 1953, while Woody was trying to build a fire at a friend's encampment, his arm ignited, injuring him severely. The accident echoed his father's fire twenty-five years earlier and marked a turning point in Woody's attitude toward his illness. For some time, it had seemed that he might be able to elude the disease simply by denying its existence, but the fire wiped all hope from his mind. The disease was advancing, slowly robbing him of his youth and autonomy, and he would never lick it. By the time Anneke gave birth to their daughter, Lorina Lynn, in February of 1954, Woody had drawn so far into his shell there seemed little cause to celebrate. The couple was broke, stuck in a cramped apartment in New York City (where they had relocated) with few hopes for the future. By year's end, their marriage had unraveled completely.

As his health steadily declined, Woody's professional reputation grew. Royalties were trickling in with some regularity, and young musicians across the country were beginning to emulate his style and repertoire. In 1956, a circle of close friends, pleased about the increasing attention being paid Woody's work and hoping to safeguard his children's financial future, established the Guthrie Children's Trust Fund. Harold Leventhal, the Weavers' manager and producer, was named a trustee, along with Pete Seeger and a union official named Lou Gordon. They were charged with publicizing Woody's contributions to the field of American music, streamlining the collection of royalties, and providing for his children's economic security. Since Woody's royalty earnings were still fairly meager in 1956, a benefit was planned to raise money for the fund.

Though many of Woody's old musical companions agreed to participate, Woody was not among the performers. His movements had grown so shaky and erratic that he could scarcely feed himself, let alone finger a guitar. He sat near the stage of Pythian Hall, where the benefit was held, and watched intently as Millard Lampell and the other Almanacs, Seeger and the other Weavers, and numerous regulars from People's Songs talked about his life and performed his music. When they began singing "This Land Is Your Land," Woody could scarcely contain himself. For a few brief moments, he forgot the horrible dead end of Huntington's

At the 1956 benefit for the Guthrie Children's Trust Fund. Woody is standing, Harold Leventhal second from right.

and was transported back over the years. He had traveled a long road, a difficult road, with many hardships still ahead. But for a little while, in the darkened hall, surrounded by friends and peers with the sound of his own lyrics filling his ears, Woody felt sublimely happy.

> *This land is your land, this land is my land,*
> *From California to the New York island;*
> *From the redwood forest to the Gulf Stream waters*
> *This land was made for you and me.*

By the time the early 1960s rolled around, Woody's fame had blossomed. It was a time of renewed interest in American folk music, an era of unusual vitality and independence. The dark years of McCarthyism were slowly receding, and the nation's young adults were beginning to embrace their cultural history. It was the rebirth Woody and Pete Seeger and Lee Hays and Alan Lomax and the others had worked so long and hard to bring about.

Although Woody was aware of the new movement, he remained largely outside it. He could no longer write or hold a guitar. Even sitting in a chair required enormous effort. For many of the young people now taking up guitars, Woody was an icon—a living legend—and they imitated him endlessly.

Some were remarkable clones. In 1961, a young guitar player and songwriter named Bob Dylan visited Woody at Greystone Park hospital in Morris Plains, New Jersey, where he had lived with constant medical attention for several years. Dylan had memorized all Woody's songs and readily admitted he was a walking "Woody Guthrie jukebox." A few years before, as Woody suffered the early symptoms of Huntington's disease, a Brooklyn youth named Jack Elliot had taken to following him around, memorizing every facet of his personality and gestures, down to the minutest pause and twitch.

In the early 1960s, it became a custom among Woody's circle of friends to have frequent weekend gatherings centered around him—most of them organized by Sidsel and Bob Gleason, a couple of long-time fans who lived near Greystone Park. Harold Leventhal, Pete Seeger and Alan Lomax would often attend, along with Marjorie and the children (Arlo was becoming an accomplished musician himself), Dylan and other aspiring young musicians. The younger people would be eager to perform for Woody, hoping to win his blessing, and the older folks relished another opportunity to be together, savoring the past and the ties between them. Even Cisco Houston materialized in early 1961, weakened by stomach cancer and obviously saddened by the decline in Woody's health, yet also moved by his courage. As the party ended and Cisco turned to leave, he stooped to kiss Woody tenderly on the forehead. It would be their last encounter.

Eventually the gatherings grew in number and began taking place in different parts of the country, but Woody was no longer present. The movement had its own momentum now, with an army of young musicians to carry the traditions forth: Joan Baez, Bob Dylan, Joni Mitchell, and Peter Yarrow, Noel "Paul" Stookey and Mary Travers (who formed the group known as Peter, Paul and Mary). In the summer of 1963, forty thousand people turned out for the Newport Folk Festival organized by Pete and others, and two years later the crowd surged to eighty thousand. By then Woody was no longer able to walk or even speak. His days passed in a succession of sameness, high-lighted only by the visits of a few steadfast friends such as Leventhal.

Marjorie was his primary salvation. She visited regular-ly, calmly wiping his chin and chatting away in her soothing voice, refusing to be daunted by the awful progression of the disease. Though Huntington's was thought to result in the total annihilation of the brain, Woody's eyes remained alert and full of feeling to the end. Marjorie was convinced he understood — and needed — every word she spoke.

He had been ill a long time, and Huntington's was winning its long assault. Woody lost weight steadily, until he was little more than skin and bones and could no longer sustain the violent spasms that had racked his body for so many years. His life was closing — it was only a matter of time.

Early on the morning of October 3, 1967, just a few hours after Marjorie kissed him good-night and went home to her fam-ily, Woody died in Creedmoor State Hospital in Queens, New York. He was fifty-five years old.

Standing, from left: Arlo Guthrie, Will Geer, Cisco Houston, Lee Hays and Millard Lampell. Seated, from left: Woody, Nora Lee Guthrie and Sonny Terry.

Epilogue

oday Woody Guthrie and Leadbelly are widely recognized as the nation's greatest folk musicians— Leadbelly for rescuing large portions of the African-American tradition from extinction, including songs from slavery, and Woody for the thousand or more ballads he created out of Anglo-American standards and the songs of the white rural southwest. Several of his creations are now classics, including "Pastures of Plenty," "So Long, It's Been Good to Know Yuh" and, of course, "This Land Is Your Land," which has been performed and recorded by a multitude of groups and individuals over the years.

Yet the versions of "This Land" taught or orchestrated today are often incomplete. In the last years of his life, Woody himself warned that the song was being oversimplified. Pete Seeger recalled Woody's efforts to pass down the complete lyrics to his son Arlo, who "was so young he could barely write." Seeger explained, "Woody got out of the hospital on the weekend to visit his family for a few hours, and he says, 'Arlo, they're singing my song in the schools, but they're only singing three verses. You got to learn the other verses.'" Then Woody took Arlo in the back yard and taught him the rest of the song—verses that reflect Woody's deep affection for the diversity and natural beauty of his homeland and convey a sense of autonomy well-suited to a nation that prides itself on its personal freedoms. Here, then, is the complete anthem:

> *This land is your land, this land is my land*
> *From California to the New York Island,*
> *From the Redwood Forest, to the Gulf Stream waters,*
> *This land was made for you and me.*

As I went walking that ribbon of highway,
And saw above me that endless skyway,
And saw below me the golden valley, I said:
This land was made for you and me.

I roamed and rambled, and followed my footsteps
To the sparkling sands of her diamond deserts,
And all around me, a voice was sounding:
This land was made for you and me.

Was a great high wall there that tried to stop me;
Was a great big sign there says "Private Prop'ty."
But on the back side it didn't say nothing—
That side was made for you and me.

When the sun come shining, then I was strolling
In wheat fields waving, and dust clouds rolling;
The voice was chanting as the fog was lifting:
This land was made for you and me.

One bright sunny morning in the shadow of the steeple
By the Relief office I saw my people —
As they stood hungry, I stood there wondering if
This land was made for you and me.

Nobody living can ever stop me,
As I go walking my freedom highway.
Nobody living can make me turn back.
This land was made for you and me.

Throughout his life, Woody was a prolific writer, authoring more than one thousand songs, an autobiography, a novel (*Seeds of Man*, published posthumously, in 1976), several songbooks, and thousands of letters, newspaper columns and miscellaneous jottings. He scribbled his thoughts, lyrics and other musings in notebooks, on napkins, in the pages of date books and diaries, on the backs of envelopes, on discarded paper — wherever he found blank space available. His thoughts were always flowing and, until he became incapacitated by Huntington's disease, his hand recorded them dutifully. Today the vast majority of his writings are preserved in the Woody Guthrie Archives in New York City, where they are being documented and organized, to be made accessible to scholars researching his life and times.

Like his most famous song, Woody himself has been oversimplified and romanticized over the years — often depicted as a blithe fellow who traveled the highways writing happy verses about America. But he seems to have had as deep a capacity for sorrow as for gladness, as well as an abiding affection for people excluded from the nation's bounty. Many of his songs arose in the moment, in response to specific issues and events, and faded away just as quickly. But in that moment they engaged and inspired his audiences by reflecting the people's strengths as well as their struggles, and by urging unity and action instead of complacence and defeat.

For Woody, music wasn't a hobby or a profession, but — as his son Arlo once explained — "a way of life." He took in the world around him, down to the smallest details, and it came out in music. He witnessed many tragedies in his lifetime, but many triumphs as well. He remained productive in the face of both. It was a matter of survival.

"You are a songbird right this minute," Woody wrote. "Today you're a better songbird than you was yesterday, 'cause you know a little bit more, you seen a little bit more, and all you got to do is just park yourself under a shade tree, or maybe at a desk, if you still got a desk, and haul off and write down some way you think this old world could be fixed....It wouldn't have to be fancy words. It wouldn't have to be a fancy tune. The fancier it is the worse it is. The plainer it is the easier it is, and the easier it is, the better it is — and the words don't even have to be spelt right."

Notes

The basic chronology of this biography, as well as many of the events it describes, were taken from Joe Klein's intricately detailed *Woody Guthrie: A Life*, which conveys the tremendous scope and intensity of Guthrie's creative years and the dramatic historical and political landscape on which he traveled. Other events, verified by secondary sources, were based on descriptions in *Bound for Glory*.

The chapters describing the origins of the Dust Bowl and the westward migration were based on Guthrie's writings, his characterizations of the period included in the *Library of Congress Recordings*, on Carey McWilliams's *Ill Fares the Land*, and on information provided by Guthrie scholar Guy Logsdon of Tulsa, Oklahoma, including his article, "The Dust Bowl and the Migrant."

Studs Terkel's *Hard Times: An Oral History of the Great Depression* and Howard Zinn's *A People's History of the United States* provided the foundation for the chapters describing social conditions in the thirties, forties and fifties. The sections on Joe Hill and the Wobblies were based, in large part, on the wealth of information contained in *Rebel Voices*. And the story of Guthrie's "wind machine" was taken from Arthur H. Landis' reminiscence, "Woodie Guthrie and the Wind Machine."

Sections describing the Almanac Singers, the Weavers, and People's Songs, as well as insights into the relationship between folk song and the labor movement in 20th century America, were based on Pete Seeger's *The Incompleat Folksinger*, his *Where Have All The Flowers Gone?*, on the Smithsonian's *Folk Song America*, and on Doris Willens' *Lonesome Traveler: The Life of Lee Hays*. Seeger's memories of the Peekskill "riots" of 1949 were quoted in Chapter 22. The Lee Hays biography provided another version of events at Peekskill, including Guthrie's comments at the time. And Seeger passed along the story of Arlo Guthrie learning the last verses of "This Land Is Your Land."

Finally, Harold Leventhal's memories of the McCarthy era and Guthrie's battle against Huntington's disease helped shape the later chapters of this biography. All sources are listed in the Bibliography. For more information about Woody Guthrie, write to Woody Guthrie Publications, 250 West 57th Street, New York, NY 10107.

Most of the quotations laced throughout these pages come from Guthrie's own writings or from the *Library of Congress Recordings*. The quotations are delineated below:

Chapter 1. "Crying Don't Help"
P. 10 "Hello there...": *Bound for Glory*, p. 134.
P. 10 "It don't help...": *Ibid.*
P. 11 "For a while, it looked like trouble....": *Ibid.*, p. 135.

Chapter 2. Town on a Hill
P. 15 "stand away out and wiggle...": *Pastures of Plenty*, p. 177. "it sounded like a song...": *American Folksong*, p. 2. "when he would call the purebred...": *Ibid.*
P. 17 "everything was nice, new...": *Pastures of Plenty*, p. 2. "Pretty soon the creeks...": *Bound for Glory*, p. 93. "for miles and miles...": *Ibid.* "He had to go to a doctor...": *Ibid.*, p. 139.
P. 18 "I'd hold both of his hands...": *Ibid.*

Chapter 3. Railroad Blues
P. 19 "Maybe it had housed somebody...": *Ibid.*, p. 143.
P. 20 "the lonesomest piece of music...": *Library of Congress Recordings*, tape 1. "never did play the same...": *Ibid.* "a feeling in me that...": *Bound for Glory*, p. 153.
P. 21 "still believed that he could start out...": *Ibid.*, p. 138.

Chapter 4. Ghost Town
P. 23 "It seemed like everything in the world...": *Ibid.*, p. 158.
P. 24 "We elected our own sheriff...": *Library of Congress Recordings*, tape 1.

Chapter 5. Boom Town
P. 27 "wilder than a woodchuck...": *Bound for Glory*, p. 162. "because the big majority of the working folks...": *Ibid.*
P. 28 "of another description": *Library of Congress Recordings*, tape 1. "I thought it sounded...": *Ibid.* "a few little old songs": *Ibid.*
P. 30 "Somewhere on the outskirts of town...": *Bound for Glory*, p. 172.

Chapter 7. Buried Treasure
P. 34 "there wasn't a high blade...": *Seeds of Man*, p. 123.
P. 35 "I'd been used to looking...": *Ibid.*, p. 121. "humpy yellow foothills...": *Ibid.*, p. 127.

Chapter 8. I'm Going Where There's No Depression
P. 39   "The dust crawled down...": *Bound for Glory*, p. 179.

Chapter 9. Dust Pneumonia
P. 41   "blackest and the thickest": *Library of Congress Recordings*, tape 1. "Just go to Amarillo...": *Ibid.*
P. 42   "Just to see a thing...": *Ibid.* "A whole bunch of us...": *Ibid.* "It got so dark...": *Ibid.* "They just said, 'This is the end....'": *Ibid.*

Chapter 10. Highway 66
P. 45   "I made up new words...": *Bound for Glory*, p. 178. "At first it was funny songs...": *Ibid.*
P. 46   "I remember a frog...": *Ibid.*, p. 243.

Chapter 11. Little Red Songbook
P. 48   "too proud": *Ibid.*, p. 201.
P. 49   "The world turned into...": *Ibid.*, p. 223. "All you have got to do...": *Ibid.* "They asked us questions...": *Library of Congress Recordings*, tape 1. "I seen things out there...": *Ibid.*
P. 52   "the old tractor setting...": *Ibid.*

Chapter 12. Lefty Lou
P. 53   "tall, thin-faced...": *American Folksong*, p. 4.
P. 57   "All the newspaper headlines...": *Library of Congress Recordings*, tape 2. "All these people didn't go...": *Ibid.*

Chapter 13. A New Deal
P. 62   "About every few feet...": *Bound for Glory*, p. 248.
P. 65   "I heard these two girls...": *Ibid.*, pp. 252-3.

Chapter 14. Woody Sez
P. 67   "I made it my business...": *Pastures of Plenty*, p. 54.
P. 68   "You've seen a million...": *Bound for Glory*, p. 249.
P. 69   "Now it looks like...": *Pastures of Plenty*, p. 29.

Chapter 15. The Big Time
P. 72   "We loaded in a taxi...": *Ibid.*, p. 34. "street cars [that] run under...": *Ibid.*, p. 45.
P. 73   "little, short fellow with a western hat...": Pete Seeger, *The Incompleat Folksinger*, pp. 42-3.
P. 74   "'Lost Train Blues' played on the harmonica...": *Library of Congress Recordings*, tape 1.
P. 75   "Had some pretty rich oil fields...": *Ibid.* "When did you make that...": *Ibid.*, tape 2.

P. 76   "He had a slow running...": *American Folksong,* pp. 11-2.

P. 78   "I never sung...": *Pastures of Plenty,* p. 242.

Chapter 16. Along the Green Valley

P. 85   "hated all of my new books...": *Ibid.,* p. 69.

Chapter 17. Railroad Pete

P. 86   "It was here that I learned...": *Ibid.,* p. 73.

P. 87   "I figured a dancer...": *Ibid.,* p. 74. "I would do all right...": *Ibid.* "smiling like they'd never...": *Bound for Glory,* p. 290.

P. 88   "If you play any part...": *Pastures of Plenty,* p. 204.

P. 89   "blew and whipped...": *American Folksong,* p. 7. "Do you know what a hoper...": *Pastures of Plenty,* p. 95. "Your mama and me...": *Ibid.,* p. 102. "Maybe I could talk to you...": *Ibid.,* p. 104.

P. 90   "There's a feeling in music...": *Ibid.,* pp. 105-6. "dancer's legs": Joe Klein, *Woody Guthrie,* p. 263.

Chapter 18. A Nautical Life

P. 94   "A torpedo knocks a lot...": *Pastures of Plenty,* p. 87. "every wall was either...": *Ibid.,* p. 134.

Chapter 19. Boot Camp

P. 98   "I hate a song that makes...": *California to the New York Island,* p. 16.

P. 99   "He must have seen me coming in": *Pastures of Plenty,* p. 154. "One reason why I have to write...": *Ibid.,* pp. 147-8.

Chapter 20. Songs to Grow On

P. 100   "Took Cathy to school...": *Ibid.,* p. 151. "How did they get you...": *American Folksong,* p. 7.

P. 101   "Will the sun shine...": *Pastures of Plenty,* p. 153. "Marjorie is small in size...": *Ibid.,* p. 88.

P. 103   "Pete walked down some...": *Ibid.,* p. 156. "who loved to sing...": Pete Seeger, *The Incompleat Folksinger,* p. 20.

P. 105   "Cathy dances only to a song...": *Pastures of Plenty,* p. 163. "I liked having Marjorie there...": *Ibid.,* p. 175. "Let your kids teach you...": *Ibid.,* p. 178.

Chapter 22. "Go Back To Russia!"

P. 108   "If your work gets...": *Ibid.,* p. 197.

P. 109   "ain't all good...": *Ibid.,* p. 78.

P. 112 "Go back to Russia!": Pete Seeger, interview, April 7, 1994. "Oh-oh. Be prepared...": *Ibid.* "about waist-high...": *Ibid.* "about as big as...": *Ibid.* "Officer, aren't you...": *Ibid.* "Move on! Move on!": *Ibid.*

P. 113 "I've seen a lot...": Doris Willens, *Lonesome Traveler*, p. 114.

Chapter 24. Green Pastures

P. 118 "I ain't neither one...": *Pastures of Plenty*, p. 173.

Epilogue

P. 124 "was so young...": Pete Seeger, interview, April 7, 1994. "Woody got out...": *Ibid.* This version of "This Land Is Your Land" is taken from Pete Seeger, *Where Have All The Flowers Gone?*, p. 142.

P. 126 "You are a songbird...": *Pastures of Plenty*, p. 64.

Bibliography

Guthrie, Woody. *American Folksong.* Edited by Moses Asch. New York: Oak Publications, 1961.

—. *Bound for Glory.* 1943. Reprint. New York: Penguin USA, Plume, 1983.

—. *California to the New York Island; Being a Pocketfull of Brags, Blues, Bad-Men Ballads, Love Songs, Okie Laments, and Children's Catcalls.* Edited by Millard Lampell. New York: Guthrie Children's Trust Fund, 1958.

—. *Pastures of Plenty: A Self-Portrait.* Edited by Dave Marsh and Harold Leventhal. New York: HarperCollins, 1990.

—. *Seeds of Man; An Experience Lived and Dreamed.* New York: E.P. Dutton, 1976.

Klein, Joe. *Woody Guthrie: A Life.* New York: Ballantine, 1980.

Kornbluh, Joyce L., ed. *Rebel Voices: An I.W.W. Anthology.* Ann Arbor: Univ. of Michigan Press, 1972.

Landis, Arthur H. "Woodie Guthrie and the Wind Machine." *The Hawsepipe: Newsletter of the Marine Workers Historical Association* X(2) (April/May 1991).

Logsdon, Guy. "The Dust Bowl and the Migrant." *American Scene* XII(1)(February 1971).

McWilliams, Carey. *Ill Fares the Land: Migrants and Migratory Labor in the United States.* 1942. Reprint. New York: Arno Press, 1976.

Seeger, Pete. *The Incompleat Folksinger.* New York: Simon & Schuster, Fireside, 1972.

—. *Where Have All The Flowers Gone?* Bethlehem, Penn.: Sing Out, 1993.

Terkel, Studs. *Hard Times: An Oral History of the Great Depression.* 1970. Reprint. New York: Pantheon, 1986.

Willens, Doris. *Lonesome Traveler: The Life of Lee Hays.* New York: W.W. Norton, 1988.

Zinn, Howard. *A People's History of the United States.* New York: Harper & Row, 1980.

Music Collections

Guthrie, Woody. *Woody Guthrie Songs.* New York: The Richmond Organization, 1992.

—. *The Woody Guthrie Songbook.* Edited by Harold Leventhal and Marjorie Guthrie. New York: Grosset and Dunlap, 1976.

Lomax, John A. and Alan Lomax. *Folk Song: USA.* Edited by Alan Lomax. Charles Seeger and Ruth Crawford Seeger, music editors. New York: Duell, Sloan and Pearce, 1947.

Audio Recordings

Guthrie, Woody. *Columbia River Collection.* Cambridge, Mass.: Rounder, 1987.

—. *Dust Bowl Ballads.* 1940. Reissue. Cambridge, Mass.: Rounder, 1988.

—. *Woody Guthrie: Library of Congress Recordings.* 1964. Reissue. Cambridge, Mass.: Rounder, 1988.

Guthrie, Woody and Huddie Ledbetter, with various performers. *Folkways: The Original Vision.* Washington, D.C.: Smithsonian Folkways, 1988.

Various performers. *Folk Song America: A 20th Century Revival.* Edited by Norman Cohen. Smithsonian Collection of Recordings. Washington, D.C.: Smithsonian, 1990.

Various performers. *Folkways, A Vision Shared: A Tribute to Woody Guthrie and Leadbelly.* New York: Columbia, 1988.

Chronology

1912 JULY 14. Woodrow Wilson Guthrie is born in Okemah, Oklahoma. He is the third of Charley and Nora Guthrie's five children.

1919 MAY. Clara Guthrie dies from burns sustained while using a kerosene iron.

1920 Oil is discovered around Okemah.

1923 Charley goes broke. He moves his family to Oklahoma City.

1924 The Guthries move back to Okemah, settling into an abandoned "boomer shack."

1926 Charley sends his two youngest children to live with his sister in Texas.

1927 Charley catches fire. Nora is taken to the state mental hospital in Norman, Oklahoma.

1929 Woody leaves Okemah, eventually heading to Pampa, Texas, to join his father. Nora Guthrie dies.

   OCTOBER. The stock market crashes, and the Great Depression begins.

1931 Woody meets and falls in love with Mary Jennings.

1932 Woody goes searching for Jeremiah P. Guthrie's silver mine. Returning to Pampa, he forms the Corncob Trio with Matt Jennings and Cluster Baker. Franklin D. Roosevelt is elected president of the United States. The drought begins.

1933 OCTOBER 28. Woody marries Mary Jennings.

1935 People begin leaving Pampa and heading west, taking Highway 66. Woody compiles his first songbook.

   APRIL 14. The Great Dust Storm hits Pampa.

   NOVEMBER. Mary gives birth to Gwendolyn Gail ("Teeny").

1936 Woody starts taking little jaunts out of Pampa, then wanders as far as California.

1937 JULY. Mary gives birth to Sue. Jack Guthrie and Woody debut on KFVD in Los Angeles.

SEPTEMBER. Woody begins a new radio show with Maxine Crissman ("Lefty Lou").

1938   JANUARY. Woody and Maxine go to radio station XELO in Tijuana, Mexico. They return to KFVD a few weeks later.

JUNE. Woody and Maxine perform together for the last time on KFVD. Owner Frank Burke asks Woody to investigate the living and working conditions of the migrants.

NOVEMBER. Culbert Olsen is elected governor of California.

1939   APRIL. John Steinbeck's *The Grapes of Wrath* is published.

MAY. Woody begins writing a column, entitled "Woody Sez," for the *People's World*.

AUGUST 23. Adolf Hitler and Joseph Stalin sign a non-aggression pact. One week later Germany invades Poland.

SUMMER/FALL. Woody and Will Geer tour the migrant camps.

SEPTEMBER. The Soviet Union invades Poland.

OCTOBER. Mary gives birth to Will Rogers Guthrie.

NOVEMBER. The Soviet Union invades Finland. Woody's relationship with KFVD's Frank Burke crumbles.

THANKSGIVING. Woody, Mary and the kids are back in Texas.

1940   Woody hitchhikes to New York City, where he writes the first draft of "This Land Is Your Land." He makes a series of recordings for the Library of Congress. In the spring, Woody performs on New York radio programs and records an album, *Dust Bowl Ballads,* for Victor Records.

1941   JANUARY. Woody flees New York in a panic, leaving his radio career in tatters. He and Mary head for California.

Back in New York, Pete Seeger, Lee Hays, Millard Lampell and others form the Almanac Singers.

EARLY MAY. Woody gets a thirty-day contract to write songs about the Grand Coulee Dam.

JUNE 22. Germany invades the Soviet Union.

JULY. Woody joins the Almanacs' cross-country labor-organizing tour.

EARLY SEPTEMBER. Woody and Mary separate. Woody returns to New York.

DECEMBER 7. The U.S. naval base at Pearl Harbor, Hawaii, is bombed by Japanese forces.

1942   Woody lands a contract to write his autobiography. He meets Marjorie Greenblatt Mazia in New York City.

FEBRUARY 14. The Almanacs perform on "This is War."

1943   Woody and Mary are officially divorced.

FEBRUARY. Cathy Ann Guthrie is born.

MARCH. *Bound for Glory* is published.

MAY. Woody wins a $1,700 Rosenwald Fellowship. He signs up with the Merchant Marines.

1944   Woody meets Moses Asch.

JUNE 6. D-Day. The Allied armies invade France at Normandy.

NOVEMBER. Franklin D. Roosevelt is elected to a fourth term.

1945   **MAY 7.** Woody is inducted into the U.S. Army, the same day Germany surrenders to the Allies.

AUGUST 9. Japan surrenders.

NOVEMBER. Woody and Marjorie marry.

DECEMBER 21. Woody is discharged from the Army and returns home to New York. People's Songs forms a few days later.

1946   Woody records children's songs in Moses Asch's studio.

1947   **FEBRUARY 9.** Cathy is badly burned in a freak accident at home in Coney Island and dies early the next morning.

JULY. Marjorie gives birth to a son, Arlo Davy.

1948   Woody writes the lyrics to "Deportee" (also known as "Plane Wreck at Los Gatos").

NOVEMBER. Henry Wallace loses his bid for the U.S. presidency.

DECEMBER. Joady Ben Guthrie is born to Woody and Marjorie.

1949   Woody's creative energy begins to dissipate.

FEBRUARY. People's Songs folds. McCarthyism begins sweeping over America.

SEPTEMBER. Woody, Lee Hays, Pete Seeger and others are attacked by a white mob at Peekskill, New York. The Weavers open at the Village Vanguard in New York City.

DECEMBER 6. Leadbelly dies of Lou Gehrig's disease.

1950　JANUARY. Nora Lee Guthrie is born to Woody and Marjorie. Leadbelly's "Goodnight Irene" becomes one of the Weavers' early hits, along with Woody's "So Long, It's Been Good to Know Yuh."

1952　Woody's personal appearance and behavior deteriorate. In the spring, he visits Okemah.

SEPTEMBER. Woody is told he has Huntington's chorea. Soon after, his marriage to Marjorie ends.

1953　Woody's arm is badly burned in a fire. He obtains a divorce from Marjorie and marries Anneke Van Kirk Marshall.

1954　FEBRUARY. Anneke gives birth to Lorina Lynn Guthrie.

1955　Woody and Anneke separate.

1956　Woody's friends establish the Guthrie Children's Trust Fund.

DECEMBER. Charley Guthrie dies at age seventy-seven in Oklahoma City. Woody writes his last letter, to Marjorie.

1959　Bob and Sidsel Gleason begin hosting weekend get-togethers in East Orange, New Jersey, for Woody and his friends.

1961　APRIL 29. Cisco Houston dies of stomach cancer.

1964　Elektra Records releases Woody's *Library of Congress Recordings.*

1967　OCTOBER 3. Woody dies in Creedmor State Hospital in Queens, New York.

Publication Credits

All drawings are by Woody Guthrie and were provided by Woody Guthrie Publications, Inc. Unless otherwise indicated, the photos on these pages were provided by the same source. In addition, the following organizations granted their permission to reprint from previously published material:

Index

A

Agricultural Adjustment
    Administration, 60, 62-63
Agricultural Workers
    Industrial Union, 38
Algeria, 94
Almanac Singers, 82-84, 87-88,
    119
American Federation of Labor
    (AFL), 61
Arkansas, 43, 45, 47, 61, 82
Asch, Moses, 95, 98-99, 105
Associated Farmers, 62-63, 68

B

Baez, Joan, 121
Baker, Cluster, 31
Bonneville Power
    Administration (BPA), 80,
    83, 107
    Grand Coulee Dam, 80-82
Bound for Glory, 89-90, 92, 105
Boydstun, Maude, 21
Brand, Oscar, 104
Burke, J. Frank, 54-56, 58-59,
    69-70, 79

C

California, 43, 45, 49-52, 72,
    75, 80
    Border control, 49
    Columbia, 79
    Los Angeles, 53-56, 63, 79,
    84-85, 107
    Migrant camps, 56, 59, 61-
    65, 67-68, 79
    San Francisco, 66, 83-84
    Scarcity of migrant jobs, 49,
    56
    Topanga Canyon, 118
Carter Family, the, 32, 39, 64
CBS radio
    "Back Where I Come
    From," 76, 78
    "Columbia School of the
    Air," 75
    "Pursuit of Happiness,
    The," 75
"Chain Around My Leg," 75
Chaplin, Charlie, 21
Civil War, 13
Cold War, 105
Colorado, 42-43

Communist party (American),
    61, 63, 66-67, 77, 98
    Daily Worker, 77-78
    People's World, 67, 69
Communists, 61, 63, 66, 69-71,
    77, 82, 88, 97-99, 104, 107-
    108, 110-111, 118
Congress of Industrial
    Organizations (CIO), 61, 83,
    111
Corncob Trio, 31-32
Crissman, Georgia, 53
Crissman, Maxine ("Lefty
    Lou"), 53-56, 58, 63
Crissman, Roy, 53
Cunningham, Agnes ("Sis"),
    83-84
Czechoslovakia, 69

D

Delaware
    Wilmington, 87, 89-90
"Deportee," 109
Dewey, Thomas, 97
"Do Re Mi," 58, 75
Drought, 37, 39, 41
Dust Bowl, 43, 49, 57, 66, 75
Dust Bowl Ballads, 75-76, 98
Dust pneumonia, 41
"Dust Storm Disaster," 42-43
Dylan, Bob, 121

E

Eastern Europe, 105
Elliot, Jack, 121

F

Fascism, 63, 83, 89
Fascists, 82, 92
Finland, 70
Folksay, 86-87
France, 69
    Normandy, 95-96

G

Geer, Herta, 72
Geer, Will, 67, 70-73, 97, 118,
    122
Germany, 68-70, 82-83, 87, 93,
    96
Gibraltar, 93
Gilbert, Ronnie, 115
Gleason, Bob, 121

Gleason, Sidsel, 121
"God Bless America," 73
"God Blessed America," 73
Gold, Mike, 104
"Goodnight Irene," 115
Gordon, Lou, 119
"Grand Coulee Dam, The," 81
Grapes of Wrath, The, 68, 75
Great Britain, 69, 72, 82
    Southampton, England, 96
Great Depression, 37-39, 60,
    97, 104
    Difficulties facing parents, 45
    1929 stock market crash, 31
Great Dust Storm, the, 41-43, 46
Great Plains, 41-42, 80
Guitar, 89, 115, 119, 121
    As source of income, 48
    Picking styles, 32
    Woody's first, 28
Guthrie Children's Trust
    Fund, 119
Guthrie, Allene, 28-29, 39, 55,
    107
Guthrie, Anneke Van Kirk
    Marshall, 118-119
Guthrie, Arlo Davy, 110-111,
    121-122, 124, 126
Guthrie, Bettie Jean
    McPherson, 32-33, 40, 45
Guthrie, Cathy Ann
    ("Stackabones"), 90, 92, 94,
    100-102, 105-108, 114
Guthrie, Charley, 10-11, 14-23,
    26-28, 32-34, 40, 45, 47
Guthrie, Clara, 9-12, 14, 18,
    44, 106
Guthrie, George, 10, 16, 21, 58
Guthrie, Gid, 35
Guthrie, Gwendolyn Gail
    ("Teeny"), 44-45, 70, 84, 110
Guthrie, Jack, 53-54
Guthrie, Jeff, 28-30, 34, 39, 55,
    107
Guthrie, Jeremiah P., 34-35, 110
Guthrie, Joady Ben, 110-111
Guthrie, Lorina Lynn, 119
Guthrie, Marjorie Mazia, 86-
    87, 89-92, 94, 99-103, 105-
    107, 110, 114-118, 121, 122
Guthrie, Mary Jennings, 32-
    33, 39-40, 42, 44-45, 50-52,
    54-55, 58, 66, 70-71, 78-80,
    83-85, 87, 99
Guthrie, Mary Josephine, 18,
    21, 33, 40, 69

Guthrie, Nora (mother), 10-12, 14-22, 25, 30, 32, 44, 106
Guthrie, Nora Lee (daughter), 110-111, 122-123
Guthrie, Roy, 9, 17-23, 34, 47, 107
Guthrie, Sue, 54, 70
Guthrie, Will Rogers, 70-71
Guthrie, Woodrow Wilson ("Woody")
And money, 44, 103
Birth, 14
Death, 122
Early symptoms of Huntington's, 114, 116
First marriage, 39
First songbook, 40
First trip to California, 48-50
Huntington's diagnosis, 117
Inducted into Army, 99
Joins Merchant Marines, 91
Mother's death, 30
Mother's departure, 22
Move to New York, 71
Move to Texas, 26
Musical abilities, 53, 66
Performance styles, 57, 67
Returns to high school, 28-29
Second marriage, 100
Third marriage, 118
Tours migrant camps, 59, 61-64, 67
Views on music, 90, 126
Writings, 125-126

H

Haaglund, Joel, 50
Harmonica, 20-21, 24, 54, 89
Hawes, Pete, 83
Hays, Lee, 82, 84, 104, 111, 113, 115, 118, 120, 122-123
Headline Singers, 89
Hellerman, Fred, 115
Highway 66, 35, 43-44, 46-47
Hill, Joe, 50-51, 64, 66
Hitler, Adolf, 63, 68-70, 82-83, 92, 99
Hobos, 48-49, 55
Hoovervilles, 63
Houston, Cisco, 67, 76, 80, 91-92, 96-97, 100, 104, 118, 121-123
Huntington's disease, 25, 117, 119, 121-122, 126

I

"I Ain't Got No Home," 64-65
Illinois
Alton, 99
Chicago, 27, 44, 52, 61, 83

Industrial Workers of the World
See Wobblies
Iowa, 43, 61
Italy, 87
Sicily, 93-94
Ives, Burl, 72, 104

J

Jackson, Aunt Molly, 73
Japan, 87
Jaw harp, 24
Jennings, Fred, 79
Jennings, Matt, 29-32, 55, 79

K

Kansas, 42-43
KFVD radio (Los Angeles), 54-56, 66-67, 69-70, 79

L

Labor unions, 60-63, 67, 77, 82-84, 97, 103, 107-108, 111-112
Lampell, Millard, 82, 84, 104, 119, 122-123
Ledbetter, Huddie ("Leadbelly"), 73, 76-77, 80, 89, 114-115, 124
Leventhal, Harold, 119-122
Lewis, John L., 61
Library of Congress
Archive of Folk Song, 74
Life magazine, 91
little red songbook, the, 48, 50-51
Lomax, Alan, 73-80, 104, 120-121
Lomax, Bess, 73, 83-84
Lomax, Elizabeth Littleton, 74
"Lost Train Blues," 74
Lou Gehrig's disease, 114
Louisiana, 76

M

Martha Graham Dance Company, 87
Maslow, Sophie, 86
McCarthy, Joseph, 118
McCarthyism, 120
McGhee, Brownie, 88-89
Merchant Marines, 91, 96, 98
Migrant workers, 25-26, 37-39, 52, 60-61, 63, 68, 73, 80-81
Living conditions, 49-50, 56-57, 59, 61-65

Mexican nationals, 50, 79, 109-110
Modes of transportation, 37, 48-49
Music of, 55
Minnesota
Minneapolis, 83
Missouri, 43, 53
Mitchell, Joni, 121
Model Tobacco Company, 76, 88
"Pipe Smoking Time," 76, 78
Mooney, Tom, 66
Moore, Amalee, 50
Moore, Casper, 24-25
Moore, Laura Guthrie, 50, 53, 55
Moore, Nonie, 25, 47
Moore, Tom, 24-25, 47
"Mr. Tom Mooney Is Free," 66

N

Nail, Sam, 35
National Maritime Union, 83, 91, 98
National Recovery Administration, 60
Nazi party, 68
Nazis, 68-69, 95
Nebraska, 43
New Deal, the, 60
New Jersey, 106
Fort Dix, 99
Morris Plains, 121
New Mexico, 42, 48
New York City, 31, 61, 70-72, 75-80, 82-83, 85-90, 95, 107, 112-113, 116, 119, 126
Bowery, 72
Brooklyn, 90
Coney Island, 94, 100, 102
Greenwich Village, 103
Hell's Kitchen, 72
Lower East Side, 72
Rainbow Room, 87
Times Square, 72
Village Vanguard, 115
"New York Trains, The," 72
New Yorker, The, 90
Newport Folk Festival, 121
"No Depression," 39
North Dakota, 42

O

Ohio
Cleveland, 83
Oklahoma, 42
Five Civilized Tribes, 13
History of, 12-14
Norman, 22, 25
Oil boom, 17, 19

Oklahoma continued
Okemah, 9, 12, 14, 17-20, 24-27, 46, 74-75, 116
Oklahoma City, 18-19, 76
Panhandle, 42
Slavery in, 13
"Old Joe Clark," 30
Olsen, Culbert, 59, 66
Oregon
Columbia River, 80-81
Portland, 80, 83-84

P

Pacifists, 82
"Pastures of Plenty," 81-82, 124
Peekskill riots, 111-115
Pennsylvania
Philadelphia, 83
Pittsburgh, 83
People's Songs, 103-105, 110, 115, 119
Peter, Paul and Mary, 121
Phonograph, the, 31
Poland, 69-70
"Pretty Polly," 81
"Preacher and the Slave, The," 51
Progressive party, 110
Prohibition, 28

R

Radio
"Hillbilly" music, 32
Advent of, 31-32
"Railroad Blues," 20
Railroad Pete, 89-90
"Riding In My Car," 101
Robbin, Ed, 66, 80
Robeson, Paul, 111, 113
Robinson, Earl, 86, 104
Rodgers, Jimmie, 32
Rogers, Will, 118
Roosevelt Bandwagon, 97
Roosevelt, Eleanor, 60
Roosevelt, Franklin D., 37, 60, 63, 97, 110
Rosenberg, Ethel, 108
Rosenberg, Julius, 108
Rosenwald Foundation, 90
Russia
See Soviet Union

S

Seeds of Man, 125
Seeger, Pete, 73, 76, 80, 82-84, 103-104, 110, 112-113, 115, 118-121, 124
Seeger, Toshi, 103
Smith, Bessie, 32
"So Long It's Been Good To Know Yuh," 46, 76, 115, 124
Social Security, 61
Songs to Grow On, 105
"Sourwood Mountain," 31
South Dakota, 43
Soviet Union, 63, 69-70, 82-83, 104-105
Spain, 93
Stalin, Joseph, 70
Steinbeck, John, 68
Stern, Arthur, 83-84
Stookey, Noel ("Paul"), 121
String bands, 30

T

"Talking Dust Bowl," 57-58
Tanner, Lee, 17
Tanner, Leonard, 18
Tanner, Mary, 17
Taylor, Claude, 39-40
Tenant farmers, 60
Terry, Sonny, 88-89, 122-123
Texas, 76
Amarillo, 35, 41
Chisos Mountains, 35, 79
El Paso, 79, 85
Galveston, 26
Lajitas, 35
Odessa, 35
Oil boom, 27, 39
Pampa, 26-27, 31, 33-34, 39-40, 42-43, 46-47, 51-52, 55, 71-72, 75-76, 107
Panhandle, 42-43
Sheppard Field, 99
Study Butte, 35
Terlingua, 35
"This Is War," 88
"This Land Is Your Land," 73, 119-120, 124-125
"This World Is Not My Home," 64
"Tom Joad," 75-76
Travers, Mary, 121
Truman, Harry, 108, 111
Tunisia, 93

U

Unemployment insurance, 61
"Union Maid," 84
Utah, 50-51

V

Victor Records, 75-76
Vigilantes, 63, 68

W

Wallace, Henry, 110
Washington
Spokane, 107
Washington, D.C., 74
Weavers, the, 115, 118-119
Whitman, Walt, 118
"Why Oh Why," 100-101
Wilson, Woodrow, 14, 51
Wisconsin, 61
Milwaukee, 83
WNEW radio (New York), 97
Wobblies, the, 38, 50-51, 61
little red songbook, 50-51
Woody Guthrie Archives, 126
"Woody Sez," 69
Work Songs to Grow On, 105
Works Progress Administration, 60
World War I, 38, 69
World War II, 69, 79, 82-83, 87, 91, 93-99, 104
German surrender, 99
Japanese surrender, 99
Normandy invasion, 95
Pearl Harbor, 87

X

XELO radio (Tijuana, Mexico), 56

Y

Yarrow, Peter, 121

WOODY GUTHRIE:
AMERICAN BALLADEER

was designed in
New York City by Eri Koizumi.

The principal type is Berthold Walbaum,
and the paper is Finch Opaque.

The book was printed and bound by
McNaughton & Gunn, Inc.,
Saline, Michigan.